The Mosaic of Islam

The Mosaic of Islam

A Conversation with
Perry Anderson

Suleiman Mourad

VERSO
London • New York

First published in English by Verso 2016
© Suleiman Mourad 2016
Foreword © Perry Anderson 2016

1 3 5 7 9 10 8 6 4 2

Verso
UK: 6 Meard Street, London W1F 0EG
US: 20 Jay Street, Suite 1010, Brooklyn, NY 11201
versobooks.com

Verso is the imprint of New Left Books

ISBN-13: 978-1-78663-212-8
ISBN-13: 978-1-78663-213-5 (US EBK)
ISBN-13: 978-1-78663-211-1 (UK EBK)

British Library Cataloguing in Publication Data
A catalogue record for this book is available from the British Library

Library of Congress Cataloging-in-Publication Data

Names: Anderson, Perry, interviewee. | Mourad, Suleiman Ali,
interviewer.
Title: The mosaic of Islam : a conversation with Perry Anderson /
Suleiman
  Mourad ; contributions by Perry Anderson.
Description: Brooklyn, NY : Verso, 2016.
Identifiers: LCCN 2016036178 | ISBN 9781786632128 (paperback)
Subjects: LCSH: Islam—History. | Islamic sociology. | Anderson, Perry. |
  Historians—Interviews. | Sociologists—Interviews. | BISAC: SOCIAL
  SCIENCE / Islamic Studies. | RELIGION / Islam / History.
Classification: LCC BP50 .A56 2016 | DDC 297.09—dc23
LC record available at https://lccn.loc.gov/2016036178

Typeset in Electra by MJ&N Gavan
Printed and bound by CPI Group (UK) Ltd, Croydon, CR0 4YY

Contents

Foreword by Perry Anderson   vii

1. The Qur'an and Muhammad   1

2. Spread of Islam and Development of Jihad   37

3. Shi'ism and Sunnism   52

4. Salafism and Militant Islam   67

Glossary   138
Short Bibliography   153
Index   156

Foreword

In the modern history of the West, there has never been a time when, for better or worse, Islam has attracted so much attention as today. There is more than one reason for that. Wars in the Greater Middle East, involving European powers and the United States, have raged for a quarter of a century, with no end in sight, and increasing repercussions in the West itself. In Europe, immigration from lands of the former Ottoman Empire has for the first time created a significant Muslim population, larger than that of twenty-two out of twenty-eight members of the EU. Transatlantic discourses of multiculturalism, encouraging concern with the plurality of religions at large, have led to greater interest in the faith historically the greatest rival to Christianity. Out of this conjunction of developments has come a considerable literature on contemporary issues bearing on Islam in the public domain. In no country, perhaps, has this production been more extensive than in France, where the work of political scientists like Olivier Roy and Gilles Keppel, and the debates to which these and other writers on topical questions have given rise, command a wide audience. In the Anglosphere, a writer like Malise Ruthven occupies the same space.

Distant from this arena lie traditions of Western historical scholarship about the Muslim world focused on its corpus of classical texts that go back to the sixteenth century. Here, France is distinguished by the continuity in its record of erudition, with a more or less unbroken line of Orientalist scholarship from the 1540s through to the present century, running from Guillaume Postel through Antoine Galland and Silvestre de Sacy to Louis Massignon or Jacques Berque and their descendants today.[1] German and Austrian studies transformed the field in the second half of the nineteenth century, with the pioneering work of Protestant and Jewish scholars like Julius Wellhausen and Ignaz Goldziher.[2] Historians based in England—John Wansbrough, Patricia Crone, Michael Cook, Martin Hinds—proved the most innovative in the third quarter of the twentieth century, before the center of gravity of Anglophone scholarship moved to the United States.[3] In such Orientalism, wherever

---

1 This characteristic emerges clearly from the leading modern history of classical scholarship on the Arab world, Robert Irwin, *Dangerous Knowledge: Orientalism and Its Discontents* (Woodstock, 2006).

2 For the extent of this tradition, see Suzanne Marchand, *German Orientalism in the Age of Empire* (Cambridge, 2009).

3 For remarks on this, Chase Robinson, "Crone and the End of Orientalism," in B. Sadeghi et al., *Islamic Cultures, Islamic Contexts* (Leiden, 2015), pp. 597–620.

it flourished, the central discipline was typically philology, in reputation one of the most specialized and least readily accessible of the human sciences. In recent years, methodological advances in the scrutiny of texts in classical Arabic, as in other languages, have produced an increasingly sophisticated *Quellenkritik*, distinguishing this world of enquiry from that of current social processes or political events.

Suleiman Mourad is a historian whose work is emblematic of this progress. Born in the late sixties to a modest Sunni family in the mountains of south Lebanon, a witness to the Israeli invasion and Lebanese civil war in his youth, he was educated at the American University of Beirut at a time when most of its students were on scholarships, and its campus was relatively free of sectarian divisions. Of his teachers, three were born in Palestine (of Sunni and Arab Orthodox backgrounds), another a Lebanese who belonged to one of the first Protestant families in the country. He completed a master's thesis on the early Arab conquests under the supervision of Tarif Khalidi, a historian averse to what he termed "Islamic triumphalism." In 1996, he was invited to pursue doctoral work at Yale University. There he immersed himself in language courses—Syriac, Persian, German—neglected at AUB, and the study of religion: Islam and mysticism, the New Testament and ancient Christianity. In 2002, he got a teaching position in Vermont, and is now professor of religion at Smith College in Massachusetts.

Out of his doctoral research came his first book, a critical scrutiny of a set of famous texts attributed to one of the most important Muslim thinkers of the generation after Muhammad, and the context of his life, showing that in large measure these—including a well-known epistle to the powerful Umayyad caliph ʿAbd-el-Malik (who ordered the construction of the Dome of the Rock in Jerusalem)—were composed long after his death, for the legitimation of later theological positions.[4] Since then, as a leading medievalist, he has written innovative studies of the interweaving in early Islamic texts of legends of Mary and Jesus, of the hermeneutic methods applied to Qurʾanic exegesis by Muʿtazila scholars under the Abbasids, and of the period and ways in which Jerusalem emerged as a central site in Muslim religious imagination.[5] Most recently, he has coauthored a pioneering examination of the historical context in which the imperative of *jihad* was reconfigured in the twelfth century, as a more unconditional duty of struggle against not only Crusaders and Mongols, but the Shiʿi rule by the Fatimids in Egypt and fellow Muslims.[6] Currently, he is looking at

---

4 *Early Islam between Myth and History: Al-Hasan al-Basri and the Formation of His Legacy in Classical Islamic Scholarship* (Leiden, 2006).

5 "Mary in the Qurʾān: A Reexamination of Her Presentation," and "Does the Qurʾan Deny or Assert Jesus' Crucifixion and Death?," in G. Reynolds (ed.), *New Perspectives on the Qurʾan*, Vols. I/II (New York, 2008/2011); "The Revealed Text and the Intended Subtext," in F. Opwis and D. Reisman (eds.), *Islamic Philosophy, Science, Culture and Religion* (Leiden, 2012); "The Symbolism of Jerusalem in Early Islam," in S. Mourad and T. Mayer (eds.), *Jerusalem: Idea and Reality* (London, 2008).

6 Suleiman Mourad and James Lindsay, *The Intensification and*

crosscurrents of tolerance in the collision between Muslim
and Christian worlds in the Near East of the later Middle
Ages. This is the *cursus* of a historian working in the most
exacting disciplinary descent of philological erudition, as it
has modernized itself.

Strikingly, however, he is at the same time not a historian detached from recent or present upheavals in the Arab
and Islamic worlds, but one in fluent command of their
contemporary political and intellectual landscapes. It is this
combination that makes Mourad so distinctive a figure, and
what he develops in this book of such interest. For here,
exceptionally, the separation between historical and topical,
philological and social, forms of understanding the Islam of
West Asia and North Africa, literatures dealing with the past
and the present, is dissolved in a single continuous set of
reflections. Beginning with the composition of the Qur'an
and its relation to Judaic and Christian forms of monotheism, it moves to the literature on the life of Muhammad,
the character of the early Arab conquests, and disputes over
succession to the position of caliph, generating the later division between Sunni and Shi'i versions of Islam. Contrary
medieval interpretations of the commandment to jihad,
from Abbasid to Crusader periods, segue into an analysis of
contemporary doctrines of Salafism. The respective fortunes
of reforming modernism and Wahhabi revivalism in recent

Reorientation of Sunni Jihad Ideology in the Crusader Period: Ibn 'Asakir
of Damascus and His Age (Leiden, 2013).

times, and the positioning of movements such as the Muslim Brothers (Ikhwan) in Egypt or the AKP in Turkey in the theological field; the reasons why the political trajectories of Shiʻi communities in Syria and Iraq have differed so markedly; the factors behind the transformation of North Africa from a once predominantly Shiʻi to a homogeneously Sunni zone; the decline of the classical schools of Islamic jurisprudence; the intensification of sectarian hostilities across the Middle East since the Iranian Revolution—Suleiman Mourad illuminates all these questions, and more, with an inimitable calm, lucidity, and candor.

The extended conversation[7] in which he does so is a product of time we spent together at the Institut d'Etudes Avancées at Nantes, where scholars from all over the world, and especially from the global South, are given a unique opportunity to learn from each other, across frontiers of discipline and country. Many conversations on the most variegated topics crisscrossed at its tables. Around these, over an unforgettable year, every sort of curiosity was aroused. This book is the fruit of one of them. Its form owes everything to the *genius loci*, and the warmth and intensity of the intellectual exchanges it generated. Without the Institute, the questions posed below would never have taken shape, nor the way they are answered given such vivid expression to the spirit of evenings by the Loire.

Perry Anderson, 2016

---

7   An earlier, shorter version of this interview was published as "Riddles of the Book," *New Left Review* 86 (March–April 2014): 15–52.

1

The Qur'an and Muhammad

When is it likely that the Qur'an was composed, and how many strata of composition does it consist of?

The Islamic tradition says that the Qur'an was revealed to the prophet Muhammad over a period of twenty-two years, between 610 and 632 CE; Muslims believe that Muhammad was not literate, and so he could not himself have produced the Qur'an. He memorized it, and a few of his followers memorized some parts of it or wrote them down. When he died in 632, there was no codex as such. Different disciples had variants written down, creating a need around the year 650 to produce a canonical version, because 'Uthman—the caliph at the time—feared these differences might cause splits among Muslims. So he put together a committee to produce a standard text for all the faithful. That is the traditional account of the origin of the written text, which was in circulation by the middle of the seventh century. We have scarcely any documentary evidence from the seventh century itself, only oral traditions whose authenticity is hard to verify, with many conflicting narratives, which makes the task of the scholar very difficult. A very few exceptions exist, such as the inscription inside the Dome of the Rock in Jerusalem (built in 692) which documents a few verses from the Qur'an (e.g., 4.171–172).

As historians, when we start examining the Qur'an, we realize that this is a very difficult text. It is not like the Hebrew Bible, and cannot be compared to the Gospels. It does not tell us the story of a person or a people. The Hebrew Bible is the story of the Israelites; the Gospels record the story of Jesus's ministry. The Qur'an is not a story of the Arabs or of Muhammad's ministry. Its unique character as a narrative poses particular problems for the historian. If we only read the Qur'an, we know very little about Mecca, Muhammad, and Arabia. Muslims have always read the Qur'an by using the books on the life of Muhammad to add historical narrative and rich details to the Qur'anic text and also to help explain what the Qur'an intends. There is nothing like it, which actually is something that the Qur'an proclaims (e.g., 18.88). Aside from some verses that address legal matters, the Qur'an has a tendency to be brief and alludes to stories, events, and issues with the assumption that its direct audience already knew them.

Some modern historians have postulated a human agent to have produced the Qur'an, but was there one author or several authors? For a long time, scholars in the field—the most influential was John Wansbrough (d. 2002)—believed that the Qur'an was finalized at the end of the eighth century or the beginning of the ninth. Since we have some early inscriptions and a recent discovery of partial manuscripts of the Qur'an that can be dated to the late seventh or early eighth century, Wansbrough's view is now discredited. The material and the type of script used tell us when these early manuscripts were written. For example, the Muslim world was by and large using paper by the middle of the eighth century, or the early ninth. Leather, papyri and parchment were abandoned because they were so much less practical. Script is also important. In the seventh century the principal scripts were Kufic (after the town of Kufa in Iraq) or the old Hijazi (after the region of Hijaz in western Arabia where Mecca and Medina are located). Later, as Muslims started to develop new styles of writing, these two scripts were abandoned. So, by and large, anything written in Kufic or old Hijazi script must come from the seventh or eighth century, especially if it is on papyri or parchment.

Where was this new manuscript evidence found?

When the Great Mosque in San'a was being renovated in the early 1970s, a secret attic was discovered above a false ceiling, containing a mass of old manuscripts. The Middle Eastern tradition (which applies to Christians and Jews as well) is that if a manuscript has the name of God or the name of the

Prophet on it, we cannot simply destroy it. The best thing we can do is put it away, or bury it, as with the Dead Sea Scrolls or the Nag Hamadeh texts. We do so not to hide them for hiding's sake, but to keep them from getting corrupted and thus insulting God. That was the case in San'a. A German scholar was allowed to study the finds, but she has published very little on them for fear of the political consequences of doing so; it seems the Yemeni government threatened Germany with repercussions if anything embarrassing appeared. But from a few of what are believed to be very early parchments in the cache, using old Hijazi script, we know that they date to the late seventh or early eighth century, and we can already see one significant difference from the canonical version of the Qur'an. The traditional story tells us there were no serious variations between the different versions assembled by Caliph 'Uthman around the year 650, though we know that down to the eighth century more popular versions of the Qur'an, without major discrepancies from the canonical text, were retained in certain regions—Iraq or Syria—out of local pride. The Yemeni manuscript, however, contains a very serious divergence. In the canonical Qur'an, there is a verse with the imperative form "say" (*qul*)—God instructing Muhammad—whereas in the San'a text, the same verse reads "he said" (*qala*). That suggests some early Muslims may have perceived the Qur'an as the word of the Prophet, and it was only some time later that his reported speech became a divine command. There is also some serious variation with respect to the length of some chapters.

One other early variation is attested. In the Dome of the Rock, three sets of verses from different parts of the Qur'an referring to Jesus can be seen (3.18–19, 4.171–172, and 19.33–36). In the original of one of these (verse 19.33), Jesus says: "Peace on me the day I was born, the day I die, and the day I am raised from death." The inscription in the Dome of the Rock, however, reads: "Peace on Jesus the day he was born, the day he died, and the day he was raised from death." Here the switch from the first to the third person is not a major change, but could be a kind of variation from the official Qur'an.

What about internal layering in the canonical version itself?

This raises a larger problem about the composition of the Qur'an as a text. There is a huge difference between the Meccan verses—those believed to have been revealed or composed in Mecca between 610 and 622—and those revealed or composed in Medina between 622 and 632. The same book contains two very contrasting styles. In the former, rhyme is key. Verses are short and rather ambiguous, with lots of references no one really understands. It has been suggested that some of these verses, especially the very early ones that are now at the end of the Qur'an, may have had a liturgical function, since they seem to involve a priest saying something and the community responding ritualistically. One term we can use to describe the Meccan parts of the Qur'an is unitarian—the verses call for a strict

monotheism that does not treat Christians and Jews as outsiders, invoking Abraham as the spiritual grandfather of all
who worship the one God. That is understandable, because
when Muhammad was in Mecca, he had no position of
leadership there. But he could win followers by railing against
Arab-style polytheism—not paganism, of which the Qur'an
is dismissive, but a polytheism where there is a main god (the
God of monotheism) whose worship has been corrupted by
the addition of other deities as intermediaries (lesser gods
of Mecca) or partners (the Trinity). In this sense, the God
of the Qur'an is an extremely biblical God—a jealous deity
who refuses to be associated with any others, insisting that if
we were to worship him, we have to worship him alone, and
if we do not, he is very vengeful.

When Muhammad gets to Medina, on the other hand, he
is no longer an average religious person. He is now a Prophet
and Statesman: the religious leader of his followers, and a
political leader in a city that includes people who do not
belong to his religious community. In Medina there were
Jews, polytheists, and new immigrants from Mecca called
Muslims. In Mecca, everybody was a cousin of everybody
else—it was one tribe of Quraysh and they had to settle their
problems by the law of the tribe. In Medina, there were different tribes unrelated to one another, different religions
and different communities. So when Muhammad becomes
head of all of them, the Qur'an suddenly assumes a different
form. It becomes less poetic, more prosaic, focusing on legal
boundaries and questions of jurisprudence, and increasingly

aggressive toward other monotheists and definitely very aggressive toward polytheism.

The division between the two components of the texts is clear-cut?

Modern scholars accept the traditional scheme that parts of the Qur'an are Meccan and other parts Medinan, though we are not always a hundred percent sure which is which. For instance, we are told of several individual verses revealed in Mecca that were included in chapters that were revealed in Medina, and vice versa. And because we do not have a clear chronology of the verses, no attempt to write the Qur'an in exact chronological order can succeed. (Two Orientalists, Theodor Nöldeke (d. 1930) and Richard Bell (d. 1952), tried to do that and only embarrassed themselves with incoherence.) The language of the text is clearly evolving, some words dropping out completely, and new ones emerging. There are also a few basic grammatical mistakes in the Qur'an — sometimes a sentence starts in the singular and ends in the plural (e.g., 9.49–50), or two particles are connected when they should not be (e.g., 3.178), or some vowels go wrong in the declensions (e.g., 22.78). This is from the viewpoint of a strict linguist. From the traditional vantage point, since the Qur'an is miraculous, these are not errors.

It is important to point out here that when the official canonical text was put together around 650, the committee opted to arrange the Qur'an in decreasing order, starting with the longest chapters and ending with the shortest. They put a short opening chapter at the beginning, and scholars in the first few centuries debated whether it was actually part of the Qur'an or not.

Are there any anachronisms in the text—if not, would that confirm an early dating of it?

If the Qur'an were from the eighth or ninth century, there would be philological traces of that. If we look at the famous Apocalypse Tapestry at Angers, dating from the fourteenth century, which illustrates the Book of Revelation (in the New Testament), in one panel the figure of a lion with seven heads holding a fleur-de-lys (representing France) faces a dragon with seven heads (representing England). Here, the Hundred Years War between France and England is projected back onto a vision formed 1,300 years earlier, and the point is to say that France was on the side of God and England on the side of the Devil. If the Qur'an was a later production, it would reflect some of the bitter disputes that broke out among the faithful once the Prophet died—major theological splits and definitely political conflicts revolving around his succession. But the Qur'an says nothing about the question of succession or any of the later schisms. So there is no reason to doubt that the Qur'an we have today is the same as the one produced in 650 and also resembles closely the Qur'an the Prophet Muhammad told his followers was the revelation he had received.

There is, however, a caveat to keep in mind. In the Arabic alphabet, there are many letters that have the same shape—what differentiates them as sounds is either the vowel that they carry, or the dots. But this was not the case in the seventh century. They had not yet invented vowels and dots for writing. For example, the three consonants *jim* (ﺟ), *ha'* (ﺣ), and *kha'* (ﺧ)—and likewise other pairs or triplets —were written using the same letter (ﺣ). Similarly, there are several other letters that are not consonantally related at all—the *ba'* (ﺑ) would have a dot under; the *ya'* (ﻱ) takes two dots under; and the *nun* (ﻥ) has one dot above—yet all have the same shape (ﺑ) when written without dots, especially at the beginning and in the middle of a word. If we have a word of four letters, and each one can have two or three ways of being read, then we have a confusing mess. Sometimes the context tells us the meaning, which makes it easier to guess how to read undotted letters. But often it does not. For example, a major difference between Sunnis and Shi'is revolves around a vowel and a hook. In one verse of the Qur'an (3.110), a word can be read either as *umma*, meaning community, or *a'imma*, meaning imams, to form "blessings on the umma" for the Sunnis, or "blessings on the imams" for the Shi'is—changing the whole dynamic of the chapter, which for Shi'is validates the institution of the imamate, whereas for Sunnis it authorizes the community to decide who rules it.

After Muhammad's death, the Qur'an was being read by people who had learnt Arabic, but were not native speakers and did not know the oral traditions behind the Qur'an. Each was proposing different ways of reading certain words. So around the year 700 another committee was assembled— this was a contribution of the Umayyad dynasty—to put in the vowels and the dots, in order to fix the text firmly so that anybody who did not know the oral Qur'an could pick it up and read it. So the *jim* is now written with a dot under the letter; the *ha'* carries no dot; the *kha'* comes with a dot above the letter.

But each side acquired a single agreed version of its own?

No, by the time of the Umayyad codification, many different ways of reading the Qur'an were already established and in circulation. So instead of causing a split among Muslims by insisting on just one reading, scholars decided in the eighth century to incorporate seven readings as canonical, and even to tolerate other less important readings as well. Ever since, there have been several canonically sanctioned ways of reading many words in the Qur'an.

Does that mean an ardent young Muslim, reading the Qur'an and wishing to master it properly, requires an apparatus explaining what the variations are?

No and yes. To make things simpler for children, texts are pro- duced according to one reading (depending on the country), which they memorize in a Qur'an school. But if we want to study and teach the text properly, we have to learn the field of exegesis, and there we are taught the variations. That became a science—any teacher of the Qur'an has to know them all. In the early twentieth century, however, a committee in Egypt produced a Qur'an for modern Muslims with the aim of unifying the world of Islam. With mass production and wide distribution, that version became pretty much used everywhere, killing off any general awareness that there are different readings of the Qur'an. In that sense, most contemporary Muslims do not understand Islam correctly, because although some can read the Qur'an, they are not aware of the way it was revealed or is supposed to be read.

When you say they can read it, surely Arabic has undergone many modifications since the seventh or eighth century?

Absolutely. Very little of the Qur'an is intelligible to an ordinary Arabic speaker today. Nor is it classical Arabic. The language of the Qur'an is in part the dialect of Mecca, in part that of other tribes of the time. It has a lot in common with pre-Islamic poetry of the late sixth or early seventh century—images, allusions, metaphors, idioms, brevity of words. This was a kind of poetry in which a horse could be invoked across a poem of ninety-four lines with a different word designating it each time—incredibly, the same word for the horse is never used twice. None of this was written down, but starting in the eighth century scholars began to commit such poems to writing as a way of explaining the Qur'an.

Classical Arabic, by contrast, is a language fabricated in Iraq in the eighth century, predominantly by Persian clerics and bureaucrats who had to administer an empire ruled by Arabs. They needed to master the language, so they started writing the first grammar books and dictionaries, which did not exist before then. So classical Arabic, because it was produced in a quite different milieu, does not give us all the knowledge that we need in order to understand the Qur'an. Modern standard Arabic is something entirely different again. It is another nineteenth-century invention, created by a committee in Egypt in the late 1800s, as a language designed to be taught in schools, with the aim of promoting pan-Arab—not Islamic—unity.

The Qur'an is often presented as the culmination of a mono-theistic tradition, with a stratigraphy of Jewish layers and Christian layers that is extremely visible. Is that correct?

In a sense, that is correct—but it is necessary to understand in what sense. For a long time, scholars would say that the Qur'an is very close to this or that passage in the Bible or New Testament, but Muhammad was a bit confused, misconstruing his sources. But now that we know better the traditions of Syriac Christianity and the Rabbinical lore, we can say that the Qur'an parallels what a Rabbinical commentator or a Christian exegete was expounding at the time on the Bible or New Testament. As I said earlier, it is wrong to compare the Qur'an to the Jewish Bible or the Gospels—we have to compare it to exegetical traditions around them in the world of late antique Christianity and Judaism. It is an engagement with living Christian and Jewish cultures, and 600 years of Christian reflection on the Jewish and Christian scriptures, or Rabbinical reflections on the Torah and Mishnah.

Muhammad lived, of course, in close proximity to Christians and Jews. But there was something particular about Mecca that can better explain the emergence of a new monotheistic creed there. This was a religious city, with a sacred shrine at its center. But it was also a commercial city, in which the logic of trade had altered its original religious practices. The elders of Mecca took the line: Why do we need to restrict worship in Mecca to our God? If we open it up and let everybody bring their own intercessory deities, or angels or saints, and put them here, then every year they will come and this will generate a lot of trade and profit for us. That will make the city more important, and better able to compete with other religious centers in Arabia. This is why the Qur'an is obsessed with polytheism. Muhammad reflects the tensions of a society where religion is felt to have been corrupted. His preaching is a call to return to an original and pure monotheism, the monotheism of Abraham. But he eventually went a little bit too far with his preaching, and when his movement looked as if it might put the well-being of Mecca at risk, he was expelled.

Once he got to Medina, the whole context changed. In the Meccan parts of the Qur'an, there are lots of positive references to Christians and Jews. In the Medinan parts, animosity against Christians and Jews surfaces abruptly in the Qur'an, in verses that are often very aggressive toward them. All of a sudden, the Muslims are commanded to fight these people. Not only should they attack their theological positions, they must wage actual war against them. There were scarcely any Christians in Medina; they did not pose any political or military threat to the authority of Muhammad. But Jews were numerous and the tradition makes clear they posed a religious and military challenge to him. That is why Muhammad ordered the massacre of one Jewish clan and expelled two others.

If one looks at two authorities on this period, Hugh Kennedy and Fred Donner, many aspects are common in their account of it.[1] But there is one point on which they appear to diverge. Kennedy says emphatically that the main form of monotheism among Arabs was Christianity but Jews were the main enemy of Muhammad in Medina, whereas Donner says there were Jews in most parts of Arabia but many more anti-Trinitarian passages in the Qur'an directed against Christians than objections to Judaism. He also observes that there is no trace of Christian asceticism in the Qur'an, whose attitude towards the pleasures and possibilities of this world is much closer to

---

1   Hugh Kennedy, *The Prophet and the Age of the Caliphates: The Islamic Near East from the Sixth to the Eleventh Century* (London, 2014), pp. 20 and 36–37; and Fred Donner, *Muhammad and the Believers: At the Origins of Islam* (Cambridge, MA, 2010), pp. 30–31 and 67–68.

what he calls the common-sense righteousness of Rabbinical Judaism. What's your view?

To some extent, I think Donner's position is more tenable. But we also need to understand what Kennedy is saying. Christianity was widespread among the Arabs in the sense that the majority of the Arabs were actually not in what is today Arabia proper. They had spread to southern Syria (what is today Jordan, Palestine, and Israel) and southern Iraq, and there they had converted to Christianity starting in the third century. The Arabs in eastern Arabia (modern Kuwait, north-eastern Saudi Arabia, Bahrain, Qatar, UAE, and Oman) were also predominantly Christians, as were many Arabs in Yemen and Najran (on the border of modern Yemen and Saudi Arabia). But in the Hijaz, where Islam emerged, there were very few Christians but lots of Jews, especially in Medina. There are many parallels to Rabbinical Judaism in the Qur'an: the need to live in observance of God's law, and enjoy what God gives the believers in moderation. There are also far more references to the Jewish Bible than to the Gospels in the Qur'an, echoing Rabbinical exegesis of it. If we compare the famous story of the binding of Isaac in the Qur'an 37.100–111 with Genesis 22, we see that in the Qur'an Isaac is a very active participant in the whole episode—he pushes his father: "Do as you are commanded and you shall find me steadfast." None of that is in the text of Genesis, but in the Rabbinical tradition of the period influences from the Christian narrative of the crucifixion of Jesus were incorporated into the story of Isaac, making him much more active, as we find in the Qur'an.[2] This is not surprising. The few archaeological digs done in Saudi Arabia have pointed to the existence of Jews in many parts of the Hijaz.

So far as Christianity is concerned, what was Muhammad's view of the Christian doctrine? The Qur'an attacks the idea of the Trinity (e.g., 5.73), and takes Christians to task for deifying Jesus (e.g., 5.116). But otherwise, its construction of Jesus's ministry is exactly the mainstream Christian position. He is described as the Word of God and the Spirit from God (4.171). The Qur'an reproduces the canonical narratives of the Annunciation of Jesus (3.45–47 and 19.16–34), and adopts one of the earliest positions on Mary's Immaculate Conception (3.35–37). There is no reference to Jesus as the son of Joseph: Jesus has no father in the Qur'an. It draws the line only at Jesus's divinity. That is what the Qur'an does not tolerate.

What is your view of Donner's argument that Muhammad was addressing a community of believers that, in his mind, was defined simply by its faith in one God as against several — rather than preaching a new creed, which would come to be called Islam?

Although questions can certainly be raised about Donner's theory, there is a lot in the Qur'an that speaks to it. We need

---

2   See, for example, the narrative in Louis Ginzberg, *The Legends of the Jews,* tr. H. Szold (Baltimore, 1998), pp. 279–86.

to understand the frame of reference. If we read the Gospel of John without knowing its historical context, we might think this was an anti-Semitic text. However, modern scholarship has found it came out of the most Jewish group of early Christians—a community that had just been kicked out of the synagogue and was reacting in anger against its expulsion. Or if we look at the books of the Prophets in the Hebrew Bible, without knowing that their authors were Israelites, we might think these people really hated the Jews. In the same way, if we go back to the Qur'an, and think of it as the writing of a monotheist who conceives himself as heir to these traditions, it is not that Muhammad is being specifically anti-Jewish here or anti-Christian there—if we are inside the tradition, and looking at what we consider transgressions against it, they will seem more pronounced than if we are outsiders. The message of the Qur'an, like that of biblical prophets, is that our duty is to live according to God's law, and if we do not, God's wrath will fall upon us. The Qur'an takes this very seriously, hence its uncompromising stance against all transgressors, including Christians and Jews.

Still, a central tenet of Judaism is that the Jews are a chosen people—others are not. Does the Qur'an touch on this?

Yes, the Qur'an actually affirms that the Jews were once the chosen people (most of Chapter 3 is exactly about that) but this changed because they rebelled against God and violated his commandments. In this respect, it parallels the Christian notion that the Jews transgressed against God so many times that God decided in the end to open the Covenant to everyone—the theology of Paul. The Qur'an certainly goes along with that openness, and, in this respect, it falls in line with a Christian influence.

The Qur'an issues one specific, clear-cut rebuke to Christians: belief in the Trinity is a lamentable deviation from monotheism. Is there any comparable point of doctrine where the Qur'an takes issue with Jewish belief?

There is one—and nobody knows where it came from. The Qur'an attacks the Jews for saying that 'Uzayr is the son of God (verse 9.30). Some scholars identify this character with Ezra, but no one really knows the origins of the belief. Otherwise, Jews are simply reproached for not living according to their law—some work on the Sabbath (verse 2.65), for example—and so disobeying the covenant they had with God. There is also something else at work, however. That is a recentering of the tradition around Abraham, and thus a downgrading of Moses. This was perfectly logical. Muhammad was in Mecca, starting a religious movement. What would he say if someone challenged his legitimacy as a true monotheist? He was not a Jew, and he was not a Christian. He was an Arab, and Arabs had never been sent prophets from God before. So he had to think of a link to the Covenant. In the Jewish tradition, all legitimacy descends from that moment when Abraham followed God and was

tested by being asked to sacrifice his son Isaac. Jewish exclusivity restricts the Covenant to a lineage: Abraham to Isaac
to Jacob and then to the Twelve Tribes of Israel. Christianity
challenged this exclusivity of descent, and opened it up. So
if we look at the genealogy of Jesus in the Gospel of Luke
(3.23–38), it shows us two issues that early Christians were
struggling with. We find that Jesus's genealogy is traced back
to Adam who, it is said, was the son of God. The theological
dilemma that the early Christians were facing was that they
too, like the Jews, are God's people; this is essentially the
argument of Paul against the exclusivity of Judaism. Another
more serious issue that we find in the Gospel of Luke and in
the Gospel of Matthew (1.1–17) is that both run Jesus's genealogy through Joseph, though one of their central theses was
that Joseph was not "the father" of Jesus and Jesus had no
human father. The question is why were the early Christians
eager to run the genealogy of Jesus through Joseph if they
believed he was not his father. The answer lies in the issue of
legitimacy: Jesus cannot be the Messiah unless it was proven
that he came from the house of David. Only Joseph pro-
vided that link. Mary was not from the house of David. She
was from the house of Aaron (the brother of Moses), and as
such was entitled to serve in the Temple as all Levites were.

That is exactly what Muhammad needed, a lineage from
Abraham in order to be part of the Covenant and thus have
legitimacy as a prophet. Hence, his genealogy was constructed
in such a way as to link him back to Ishmael, Abraham's son
not by his wife Sarah, but by his concubine Hagar. For the

Rabbinical tradition, only Isaac and his son Jacob counted. If you were not a descendant of Jacob, you were not part of the Covenant (although some rabbis were interested in the fate of Ishmael and considered him in the Covenant). Now, a new scripture had come to a descendant of Ishmael, and the Qur'an seems to emphasize that it was sent to the Arabs. Even though its message is addressed beyond the Arabs to everyone else, in several places the Qur'an (e.g., 2.151 and 42.7) makes it clear that God has now come to the Arabs, a people that he never fully engaged before.

Donner stresses that the term "Muslims"—meaning "those who submit"—is used very little in the Qur'an—the preferred term is "believers." He contends that for Muhammad submitting and believing were not the same thing. Submission was for polytheists, belief was for all monotheists, including Christians and Jews who already believed in one God. His implication is that Muhammad's project was not to create any separate religion, but simply to unify a community of believers.[3] Do you think that is correct?

I would agree, with some reservations. I think that Donner is right that at the outset Muhammad's project in Mecca was not to start something totally new. But in Medina, he confronted a need to define not only the rules governing his own followers, but also his own community's relationship

---

3   Donner, *Muhammad and the Believers*, pp. 70–2.

with those who were not members of it. This is where we start seeing the first signs of a change. Once he died, it was easy for his followers to say, these are the teachings of a new religion. With the subsequent Arab conquests came direct confrontation with the world of Byzantine Christianity and the Zoroastrianism of the Persian Empire, which gave rise to more clear-cut doctrinal definition. But as far as we can tell, for at least half a century, there was no eagerness to make or accept conversions in the territories conquered by the Arab armies. That fits with a sense that the early Muslims were part of a community of believers already, not bearers of something very new.

It is not until the reign of the fifth Umayyad caliph 'Abd-el-Malik (685–705) that serious steps were taken to make Islam something very distinctive. An example, which has received little attention from scholars, is the attestation of the faith—what in Arabic we call *shahada*. All examples of the shahada that we possess from inscriptions, coins, or papyri of the seventh century—even the inscription in the Dome of the Rock—read: "There is no God but God, one with no partners." No monotheist of any kind could object to that. 'Abd-el-Malik ordered new coinage to be issued that read, "There is no God but God, Muhammad is the messenger of God." No Christian or Jew would accept that. This was an Islamic credo intended to separate Muslims from other monotheists and proclaim their superiority over them. Later, Shi'is would develop their own shahada, which has three parts: "There is no God but God, Muhammad is the messenger of God, and 'Ali is the friend of God." The formula is meant to distinguish who is a Shi'i and who is not.

Was not 'Abd-el-Malik also seeking to create a new legitimacy for Umayyad rule, after the civil wars that had split the Muslim world in the preceding decades?

Absolutely. Coming to power as a counter-caliph in 685 with no legitimacy whatsoever, 'Abd-el-Malik championed a new project of Islam to gain acceptance of his rule. In Jerusalem — we often forget this — he deliberately built the Dome of the Rock on the site of the Temple of Solomon. This was a way of saying: we Muslims are now the more powerful, we are the heirs of Judaism whose legitimacy reverts to Islam. His strategy was a combination of Arabization — making Arabic the language of the empire — and Islamization — creating an exclusive Islamic identity to make all Muslims follow the same pattern. He also sought to promote himself as God's Caliph, rather than as a successor to the Prophet. The term caliph means successor, and before him everybody used it to mean a successor of Muhammad, with a lesser theological implication. 'Abd-el-Malik hired poets to go around celebrating him as God's Caliph in every sense.

This set in train a whole array of consequences, which tells us something about how far Muhammad perceived himself as starting a new religion and how far this was a subsequent development of his followers. If we look at the evolution of Islamic jurisprudence, the *Shari'a*, we see a very striking phenomenon: the first four caliphs—this may sound a bit shocking—by and large did not give much consideration to what the Prophet said. They did not have to clutch their heads and say, I wonder what the Prophet thought about this or would have done about that? They gave their own rulings, which more often than not were in direct contradiction to what the Prophet said or did. Some Muslim jurists in the first two centuries of Islam did the same.

For example?

There is the case of whether all creatures of the sea are edible or not. The Prophet supposedly said they were, except for the frog. The first caliph, Abu Bakr (r. 632–634), said everything is permissible. Abu Hanifa (d. 767), who established what became the Hanafi school of law, said only fish. No Muslim jurist would dare say that only what the Prophet said is Shari'a and the other statements are not. Each position has its place in the body of Islamic jurisprudence, so as Muslims we have the choice of taking the word of the Prophet, of Caliph Abu Bakr, or of jurist Abu Hanifa. There are larger contradictions than this. For instance, the Qur'an tells us that marriage for pleasure—*mut'a*—is acceptable and per-missible (verse 4.24). When warriors went out to fight, they could contract carnal unions with women for a period of a week, in a kind of formal marriage that was annulled after a few days. Caliph 'Umar (r. 634–644) banned this practice. So Sunnis do not practice it because 'Umar forbade it, even though the Qur'an allows it. Then there is the punishment for adultery. The Qur'an says the penalty is a hundred lashes (verse 24.2), but in Shari'a law it is stoning, which is in line with Jewish tradition. If the Qur'an is a revealed text whose prescriptions Muslims should adopt, why is there so much in Shari'a that is contrary to the Qur'an? The answer is that for Muslims, the Qur'an is actually not the number-one source of guidance for conduct. For most Sunnis, it is the *Sunna* of the Prophet that reigns supreme, which is spread across various massive compilations, and is complemented with an even bigger body of opinions by major early figures sanctioned by Sunnism. So even if a Qur'anic ruling contradicts the Prophet, it does not matter—the corpus of Sunna is what matters. The Shi'is follow the teachings of their imams, who are believed to receive direct inspiration from God.

How does that square with the idea that the Qur'an is not the teaching of Muhammad, but directly the word of God? Do not God's pronouncements override any human word?

That is not how it came to work within the Muslim world. Symbolically, the word of God is definitely what counts. Actually, however, it is striking that all the movements that rose to argue that the word of God trumps everybody else's got marginalized in Islam—every single movement of this kind was a failure. For Shi'is, what counts are the words of the imams. For Sunnis, it is the larger body of sayings of the Prophet, his companions, their successors, and a few later key scholars. So whereas the Qur'an can be treated quite flexibly, the imams and the Sunna become untouchable — if one starts questioning or doubting them, the whole system collapses. That is partly why cartoons that ridicule Muhammad invariably generate violence in the Muslim world.

All theological texts are rife with contradictions — the four Gospels do not agree with each other; the Pentateuch is a mass of discrepancies. How coherent is the Qur'an itself?

Coherence is a modern criterion. Any medieval text is full of contradictions. When a writer makes a case, he musters all the arguments needed to support it, and then he moves to another topic, using arguments to make a case that might contradict what he said a few pages earlier. So there are plenty of contradictions in the Qur'an, and in basic laws supposedly derived from it. Is alcohol banned in the Qur'an or not? Ultimately, Shari'a says it *is* banned. Whereas the Qur'an tells us that wine was created by Satan (verse 5.90), and then in another verse (16.67) says God created dates and grapes to be enjoyed as alcohol or as food. So God is the creator of alcohol, and Satan is the creator of alcohol. The scholarly tradition tried to make sense of some of the contradictions, but its solutions are not always logical or non-divisive. Does the Qur'an preach predestination or free will? Muslim scholars have disagreed on that, and we can list verses in support of either position. That goes for pretty much everything else in it. The theology of the Qur'an speaks to the moment, rather than to one uniform position across twenty-two years of different experiences and different engagements in Mecca and Medina. It reflects the circumstances of each situation in that span of time, and their contradictory requirements.

Looking at the overall religious message of the Qur'an, what are the fundamental tenets it passed to the faith that became Islam?

There are major pillars of Islam as prescribed in the Qur'an. The unity and singularity of God is the absolute touchstone. One also cannot be a believer, and by extension a Muslim, without believing in angels, for without angels there is no communication between God and humanity and the validity of scripture is in doubt. Nor can one be a believer without accepting the prophets who came before Muhammad and the messages they brought. One cannot be a monotheist without believing in the reality of the resurrection of the dead and the Day of Judgment. All these are musts. Then, one's duty as a monotheist is to abide by God's law, which the Qur'an does not fully define. Shari'a, however, is defined a little differently according to each school of law in Islam (five in Sunnism and a few in Shi'ism). It is Shari'a that tries to further define the tenets of Islam, and many came to believe that Islam is based on five pillars that include prayer, fast, payment of alms (*zakat*), and pilgrimage to Mecca. Such a prescription has no trace in the Qur'an. It represents an Islam identified by well-to-do male scholars that focuses primarily on orthopraxy (rituals). Moreover, nowadays, the variations within Shari'a are less clear to Muslims, but a hundred years ago someone would not say, I am Muslim, period—instead it would have been, I am Hanafi Muslim, I am Shafi'i Muslim, I am Imami Muslim.

Part of the reason why there is so much chaos in the Muslim world today is that most people do not know what Shari'a is. For there is no one Islamic Shari'a—each school of law defined its own, and one followed Islam according to the Shari'a of his/her school. It touched almost every aspect of life. For example, when someone dies, they must be buried according to the Shari'a of their school. If the burial ritual was not observed, it was a huge affront to the deceased. Nowadays, all of this is obfuscated and unclear. Many people just say, I am a Muslim, and claim they follow Islamic Shari'a. But what is Islamic Shari'a? Where do we find it? They have no clue. They are liable to think Shari'a is defined in the Qur'an, which is not true, or by some cleric or other. But what if one is from Pakistan and this cleric is from a school of law that is not practiced in Pakistan? The eclectic practices in the modern Islamic world are more a reflection of chaos rather than actual observance or clarity about what Islam is.

You mentioned the eschatological component in the message of the Prophet—the belief that a day of judgment is coming, not far off—on which some scholars lay considerable emphasis. What is your assessment of this?

This is one of the themes where we can see an evolution within the Qur'an. In the Meccan parts, it is much more pronounced. The eschaton as the End of Time is a trope that works only if it strikes at the imagination of the listeners as their last chance: Judgment Day is around the corner, and unless you repent now, you are doomed. In the Medinan period, Judgment Day remains a reality, but has become more remote. I say this because there is one very puzzling feature in these parts of the Qur'an. The one area of the law that is prescribed in incredibly minute detail is the law of inheritance (verses 4.7–12). If a movement is obsessed by the end of time, why would it go to such pains to lay down exactly how an inheritance is to be divided? Not just, give your inheritance to your son, or if you have a daughter, then a half or a quarter to her, but—what does the mother get? What does the father get? What if only women survive? Many different scenarios of inheritance are envisaged. This is clearly not a community living in panic before an imminent day of judgment. The shift is very like that in late first-century Christian writings, when the realization dawned that the new Jerusalem was not coming—we cannot keep waiting for it, we have to live, so how do we live as Christians? The focus of the tradition changes, and I think this happened fairly rapidly within Muhammad's lifetime, rather than after his death. Once he moved to Medina, he became a ruler, and the religious dynamic altered. He was no longer struggling to unify a community with an eschatological warning; he could use political force to impose his will. At that point, the Day of Judgment becomes an afterthought rather than a main focus.

What biographical evidence do we have about the life of Muhammad himself?

The earliest biography—*Sira* by Ibn Ishaq (d. 768) of Medina —is from the middle of the eighth century, though we have no copy of it. The work he composed is preserved only in quotation in ninth-century histories, or as some kind of totality by a writer who essentially plagiarized most of it some eighty years after Ibn Ishaq's death. It is likely that he produced a first version, then acquired new information and changed certain stories, often making them longer. Ibn Ishaq's style was very interesting. He would bring lots of different reports together and with great skill weave a story out of them, producing a coherent narrative that was quite new and unlike what was circulating before. In this respect, every biographer of the Prophet created a fresh portrait of him, because although some of the basic materials (anecdotes and short narratives) came from earlier sources, the collage each biographer made of them offered a different icon of Muhammad.[4] Ibn Ishaq produced an image of the Prophet of which previous generations had no inkling. Later, other writers—using oral traditions—introduced miracles into the Prophet's life or

---

4   As shown in Tarif Khalidi, *Images of Muhammad: Narratives of the Prophet in Islam across the Centuries* (New York, 2010).

mystical reflections, generating a figure who was not there in Ibn Ishaq. So while nothing certain can be said about the life of the Prophet, we can be certain that a process of glorification began not long after his death, and Muslims continued to embellish it, as new movements needed to construct an image of a Prophet closer to what they preached and believed, or even envisioned, that the life of a prophet should look like. So we suddenly start seeing in the ninth and tenth centuries—and ever since—biographies that depict the Prophet as a mystic. We do not have any before the ninth century, and even in the ninth century there were mystics who acknowledged that Muhammad was not one of them. But once mysticism became popular in the Muslim world, the Prophet *had* to be made into a mystic. More recent biographies portray Muhammad as a champion of human rights, feminism, democracy, etc., such as in the well-known *Life of Muhammad* (originally published in 1933) by the Egyptian Muhammad Husayn Haykal (d. 1956).

In much the same way, but a bit earlier, Muslims started to collect stories of miracles attributed to Muhammad. If we look, for example, at one of the most influential biographies of Muhammad by Qadi 'Iyad (d. 1149), who lived in medieval Spain and Morocco, he advocated that "no prophet ever performed any miracles that our prophet did not also perform." Yet the Qur'an affirms that while the Jewish prophets and Jesus performed many miracles, Muhammad did none (e.g., verses 17.90–94). The only so-called miracle of Muhammad is the transmission of the Qur'an. So why should there exist biographies of the Prophet full of miracles? Because in a Christian milieu, a prophecy is verified by acting out miracles (like Jesus). When preaching to Christians or debating them, Muslims had to turn Muhammad into a miracle worker in order for his prophethood to be credible.

Every biography of Muhammad is thus shaped by the agenda of its author. Once Islam began to crystallize as a distinctive religion in the late Umayyad and early Abbasid period, the first thing it needed was a story of the Prophet. The Qur'an does not give us that. But, more importantly, there is a scripture in need of an interpretation, which can only be done by recounting how the Prophet received it. That is why the *Sira* was invented—to provide a chronology of the Prophet, and to help explain the Qur'an.

Think of the development of Christianity. Paul saw no reason to write a narrative life of Jesus. It was another twenty years before the Gospel of Mark was written, around 70 CE. That was the time when Christians started to ask, who was this Jesus of Nazareth? Before that, they were all his followers, or the followers of his followers. Now, there were people in Rome and elsewhere who had never heard of Palestine—they had never been there, knew nothing about it, and needed to be told. So in the evolution of any religious movement, a point arrives where such information becomes crucial. Hence the Gospels. Then, in the second century, Christians started to wonder: what about Mary? Who was she? So we get the *Protevangelium of James*, followed in due course by Gospels of Jesus as a child, in a kind of natural progression. The *Sira* is exactly the same, as Muslims started to ask toward the end of the seventh century and the beginning of the eighth century: Who was this Muhammad? Where did he live and what was his life like? The demand produced a supply, also with an eye toward the interpretation of the Qur'an.

That is why, without the *Sira*, which is full of historiographical problems, we cannot understand the Qur'an. Countless Muslim modernists in Egypt, India, and elsewhere wanted to go Protestant-style, *sola scriptura*, just by the Qur'an as God's word. But they all realized that they have no recourse to understanding the Qur'an on its own without the biographies of the Prophet. Thus all the problems of classical Islam were brought back into modern Islam. The Prophet was a man of the seventh century, and the different medieval books on his life presented him according to the consensus of pre-modern ideals. Now we are living in the twenty-first century. His medieval biographies say that he married fifteen women, including very young girls (and at one point he was simultaneously married to nine), and did many other things that by the standards of today are considered illegal or immoral.

Within this body of literature, are there any significant disputes about the life of the Prophet?

Oh yes. We do not know when he was born. We do not know what was the first revelation he received—different sets of

Qur'anic verses are given (96.1–5 and 74.1–2). We do not know where he was when he received the revelation. Did he go to Jerusalem in the flesh, or in spirit, or in a dream? Did his Ascension to Heaven happen in Mecca or was it the same as his Night Journey to Jerusalem? In modern Islamic textbooks we have a canonical narrative, or at least a very much more harmonized one; but in classical Muslim narratives, this is not the case. Aside from the broad picture, many details cannot be ascertained. Shi'is have their own versions of the *Sira*, which Sunnis reject. For instance, there is the story of an encounter toward the end of Muhammad's life, where he put his hand on 'Ali's shoulder, passing the mantle of leadership to him with the words "He who takes me as his lord, to him 'Ali is lord." Due to its political implication, one can see how such an episode becomes an issue of contention between Shi'is and Sunnis. Shi'is affirm that it happened. Sunnis deny it ever happened, or deny that Muhammad said what he said, or that he put his hand on 'Ali's shoulder. Since we have very little in writing from the seventh century about Muhammad, we are at the mercy of oral traditions patched together from the eighth century onwards, including Ibn Ishaq's attempt to blend them into continuous narratives. But because so many scholars attempted to do the same, we now have many variations on his life, and a confusing picture.

The other major component of tradition are the hadiths. How did they arise?

The *hadiths*, or sayings attributed to the Prophet Muhammad, represent the raw material out of which the Sunna is mostly formed. We refer to it as Hadith, that is, the massive body of hadiths. In Shi'ism, the Hadith includes what the imams said and did. In Sunnism, the Hadith is complemented by a large body of anecdotes and sayings attributed to other major early Muslim figures. Consequently, when we say Sunna and Hadith, we have to factor in this large corpus that historically speaking is not by Muhammad. The Hadith has a major legal relevance and helps answer a lot of questions. If the question is about drinking alcohol, what did the Prophet and his companions or imams say about that? And the Muslims had so many questions: Can one break his/her fast during the day? When entering one's home, should he/she step in with the left or right foot? What day and time of day is best to cut one's nails? And the Hadith purportedly tells what the Prophet and his companions or imams said or did about each of those issues.

So the Hadith was needed to specify the Shari'a. Different groups started collecting hadiths perhaps as early as the late seventh century. But the collections proliferated on a large scale toward the end of the eighth and beginning of the ninth centuries. A famous legal scholar named Shafi'i (d. 820) emphasized that Shari'a and the way Muslims live must be defined according to the rules of the perfect man, Muhammad, since only he had practiced Islam flawlessly. Hence, what comes first is his Sunna: what Muhammad said and did, and how he lived. If an issue is not addressed in the Hadith of Muhammad, one must look to the Qur'an, to see if it addresses the issue. After these two sources, other factors are considered. If Muhammad and the Qur'an disagree on an issue, the Muslim must follow what Muhammad said or did, for the belief is that his Sunna too comes from God. Obviously, Muslim scholars did not tolerate the idea that the Hadith and the Qur'an might disagree. Once Shafi'i defined right living in this way, it became urgent to collect or to invent as many sayings as possible and attribute them to the Prophet. Then volumes and volumes started to be collected of what are labeled good hadiths, and efforts were made to discount fabricated hadiths. What also happened is that a large number of sayings by companions and their notable followers were also ascribed to the Prophet on the basis that they must have followed his model or heard whatever they said or did from him. So the Hadith became a vast body of lore, much of which must have been invented, since it speaks to problems within the Muslim community— political succession, free will vs. predestination, and a great deal else—that arose only after the death of the Prophet.

The authenticity of this lore was never contested?

Oh yes, many medieval scholars were liable to be called liars and accused of fabricating hadiths. In theory, there was a strict science of Hadith scholarship to sort the wheat from the chaff. An informant might be trustworthy, but if his/her hadith has only one line of transmission back to the Prophet, it cannot be depended on too much—it is called singular; or another informant might have forgotten the name of the person who told him/her the hadith—and that introduces some weakness into it; or sometimes the forger of a hadith and chain of transmission to the Prophet can be detected, since we know he never met the person he claimed to have met and from whom he heard the hadith; and so on. Some collections that were made of hadiths excluded those deemed unreliable, but other collections listed everything. The true, verifiable hadiths are called *sahih* (sound). They are relatively few by comparison to the vast number of hadiths in circulation. When Bukhari (d. 870) compiled his collection in the ninth century, he confessed that out of around 70,000 hadiths he examined, he could only authenticate as sound some 4,800—not even 10 percent. It took three or four centuries before such recensions acquired authority, when they became required reading in the curricula of seminary schools. Before that, every important scholar of Hadith would produce his own collection. The advantage of Bukhari and a few scholars like him was that their compilations were relatively small in size. The collections of later scholars became larger and larger, with less and less verification. Once a hadith was put in circulation, irrespective of its authenticity or soundness, it was ultimately accepted by some scholars.

2

Spread of Islam and
Development of Jihad

If we look at what are usually called the Arab conquests, there appears to be a notable gap between a very ecumenical faith, as portrayed by Donner and others, and the stunningly rapid expansion of the faith by force of arms. There seem to be two principal versions of what may have happened. One, which you find in Donner, argues that only minimal fighting can have occurred, since there is no archaeological evidence for much destruction in this period—there may have been some violent episodes, but only in passing, and if there was some plundering it was perhaps mainly by brigands. For a historian like Kennedy, by contrast, the expansion of Islam was rooted in the dynamic of Muhammad's unification of the Arabian Peninsula itself, where the whole mode of Bedouin existence depended on tribal raids in which every male was by definition a warrior. Once the tribes were united in a common faith, so his case goes, such raids were no longer permitted, and the dynamic of Bedouin warfare was projected outwards into a sweeping series of external conquests. In a third version, a variant on the Kennedy position, which you find in Patricia Crone, the novelty of Islam was the marriage of the idea of a universal faith with a universal empire—there had been universal conquerors, like Alexander or others, before, but they did not bring a faith, and you had universal faiths before, notably Christianity, but disconnected from the idea of a universal empire.[1] Common to all these authorities is that the conquests preceded any mass conversions, and that it is only toward the end of the ninth century that a majority-Muslim population came into being in today's Middle East. What is your view of the balance between these interpretations?

It was long customary to speak of the Islamic conquests, but now we realize that this is a misnomer. They were Arab conquests, or Arabo-Islamic conquests. Muhammad had accomplished the unification of Arabia mostly by force—tradition made no secret of this—and in some instances through alliances. When the Prophet died, new alliances were capable of reshaping the peninsula, so Abu Bakr sent his generals to enforce the recently established unity on tribes that were now taking the chance to resist it. But as an astute leader, he then turned the anger that his campaigns

---

1 Donner, *Muhammad and the Believers*, pp. 106–18; Kennedy, *The Prophet and the Age of the Caliphates*, pp. 21–2 and 58–9; and Patricia Crone, "Jihad: Idea and History," *OpenDemocracy* (1 May 2007).

aroused outwards—unleashing Bedouin energies on territories beyond the peninsula. In this respect, what became
the Arab conquests resemble nomadic conquests throughout
history, down through Mongol and Turkic times, in which
the primary motivation of mounted warriors is plunder.
What attracted the majority of Arab fighters was simply the
prospect of loot—they did not have in mind to become the
new universal lords of the known Ancient World. In this
respect, Crone's view is untenable since it reflects a much
later development, from the Umayyad and Abbasid eras,
when Muslims saw themselves as lords of massive regions
and as promoting a religion for all of mankind. Universal
religion and universal power were not yet factors at the time
of the Arab conquests.

It so happened that Arab raiders started to ride out from
the peninsula at a time when the two main superpowers of
the Ancient World, the Byzantine and Persian empires, were
exhausted by half a century of intense conflicts between
them, consuming their energies and finances in a series
of wars, aggravated by religious disputes and palace coups
within. So the Arabs descended on areas where the populations were eager for some kind of stability, and for the most
part found societies ready to tolerate their rule rather than
remain under Sassanid or Byzantine oppression. That does
not mean that the conquerors were unconcerned with booty.
But in the fertile territories and rich cultures of Palestine,
Syria, Egypt, Iraq, and Persia, the logic of raiding changed.
Here it was not a question of attacking another desert

tribe and making off with the spoils. These were communities and cities capable of paying them much more than could be gained by simply looting them. When the Arab armies reached Damascus, there are two traditions—that they seized it by force, or that they entered peacefully in exchange for payment. Probably it was a mixture of the two, but the take-over largely occurred without a major battle. Jerusalem was conquered by peace in return for payment. Most of Egypt fell in the same way. The principal exceptions seem to have come in Iraq and Iran, where fragments of the Sassanian army put up more of a fight. But there a religious factor probably kicked in. Arab conquest met less resistance in Syria or Egypt, because the religious beliefs of the conquerors—this would fit Donner's argument—were so close to those of the communities conquered. Iraq was predominantly either Christian or Jewish at the time, but under the control of a Persian empire whose Zoroastrian cult did not fit really in the universe of monotheism.

We have a reflection of that contrast between the methods of conquests in Islamic law. For the most part, land in Syria and Egypt did not technically become the property of the Muslims—it remained the property of the local populations, who owed the Muslims a tax, the *jizya*. But in Iraq and Iran the land was owned by the Muslims, because they conquered these areas by force. This is a strong indication that, elsewhere in the Middle East, the Arab conquests were accomplished with relatively little violence. Donner is right to point to the absence of any archaeological evidence of widespread destruction—which is amazing given the magnitude of the military take-over. It was long assumed that certain strata of destruction (especially in Palestine and Egypt) were the work of Arab armies, but these proved on examination to come from the Persian conquest of 614. The Arab conquests are better envisaged as the spreading out of warrior tribes from the peninsula, which was probably suffering overpopulation, along lines that were initially quite traditional, but then they came up against a social and intellectual landscape they were not ready for.

When the Arabs arrived in the Fertile Crescent and Egypt, they realized that they were a minority—not only a religious but an ethnic minority—in the regions they now had to rule. They did not want to go back to Arabia. Mecca was largely abandoned by its tribe, whose members left for Damascus, for Egypt, for Iraq. Very few of the original inhabitants stayed in either Mecca or Medina, and the same held true for many other settlements. Arabian society and economy did not offer much—the peninsula was arid, people were poor—whereas now they could enjoy the palaces and luxuries of the two empires they had inherited. Why go back to the desert? So the Arabs settled down in their conquests, aware they were an ethnic, linguistic, and religious minority in them. Tradition tells us that in this period they banned conversion to Islam, and in some cases, especially in Iraq, they charted their own separate towns and neighborhoods. This shows how little the conquests were religiously motivated: the very opposite of the stock Western image of warriors holding the

Qur'an in one hand, and the sword in the other—actually, since we can only hold the Qur'an with our right hand, all of these Arab fighters would have had to have been left-handed. In reality, the populations of Syria, Egypt, and Iraq remained predominantly Christian—there was also a significant Jewish presence—down to the ninth or tenth century. Iranian society remained, at a local level, mainly Zoroastrian or Christian until the ninth century. When conversions came, they were not under compulsion, but rather out of convenience—to get access to posts in the administration or army, or to all kinds of services and jobs that were easily accessible if one was a Muslim.

How did the concept of jihad figure, if at all, in the conquests? Crone speaks of "missionary warfare," contending that the highest duty of the faithful was to fight for Islam. Do you regard this as mistaken?

Our only evidence for the original use of jihad comes from the Qur'an, where the term, and derivatives of its root *j–h–d*, can mean either of two things: to make an effort, or to fight in the path of God. The first indicates striving in any endeavor—one makes an effort to study, or to be a good person; "making an effort" is the basic meaning of the term in Arabic. But the term also has a religious meaning, which has become idiomatic: to struggle in the path of God—often by waging war. It is there from the start. When the Qur'an uses "jihad" in this sense, the context is invariably warfare to deal with a danger threatening the Muslim community. The recent advocacy that jihad in Islam means internal struggle is a disingenuous argument to say the least. In Medina, where Muhammad came under attack and hit back, jihad was an ideological response to the challenges he faced. That does not mean it was necessarily defensive—it was the product of reciprocal hostility between the Prophet and his opponents.

By contrast, the Arab conquests are not typically described in our sources as jihad—they are called *futuh* in Arabic, which is the literal term for conquests. Yet another term again was used for the campaigns under Abu Bakr to bring disaffected tribes back to the covenant that they had signed with the Prophet, after his death—this was war against apostasy, *ridda*. But once the center of the Muslim world moved north to the ancient Near East, and the Umayyads came to power in 661, an expansionist Arab Empire was created that clashed with Byzantine power and remnants of the old Sassanian Empire, dispatching forces into Afghanistan, North Africa, and even Spain. This was no longer futuh: it was now jihad. Some good modern studies have examined the Umayyad Empire as a jihad state, unleashing a new kind of clash between the world of Islam and the world outside Islam.[2] Religious scholars converged to give legitimacy to this type of expansionist jihad, which they envisioned as

---

2   As, for instance, Khalid Y. Blankiship, *The End of the Jihâd State: The Reign of Hishâm ibn Abdelmalik and the Collapse of the Umayyads* (Albany, NY, 1994).

occurring between the Abode of Islam (*dar al-islam*), which is the Abode of Peace, and the Abode of War (*dar al-harb*). These concepts did not exist before. Religious scholars also reimagined the Arab conquests in order to employ them as foundational narratives intended to legitimize the new jihad. When the Umayyads ceased pursuing jihad, they lost their legitimacy and power in 750 to the Abbasids.

But this does not mean that the Umayyads were not pragmatics. ʿAbd-el-Malik, the fifth Umayyad caliph, was forced at the beginning of his reign (between 685 and 692) to pay the Byzantines not to attack him, and to concede territory to them, in a reversal of the pattern of Muslim expansion, because he was preoccupied with fighting internal Muslim opponents. Nonetheless, Umayyad jihad policy gave rise to a new preemptive vision of jihad, requiring virtually annual expeditions against the infidels. After ʿAbd-el-Malik, some religious scholars on the payroll of the Umayyads argued that the caliph had an obligation to conduct a jihad campaign once a year, but the damage was already done and many voices were raised against Umayyad culpability. When the Abbasids overthrew the Umayyads in the mid eighth century, they found the huge empire they inherited hard to govern, and the jihad campaigns too costly and distracting. Not wanting to be bullied into them by scholars, they hired their own scholars to redefine jihad as a collective, not an individual, duty. This transformed the practice. To give an example: prayer is an individual duty—a father cannot do it on behalf of his son. Each person has to do it for themselves.

If not done, it is a transgression against God, and the person at fault incurs a penalty. Bakery, on the other hand, is not an individual duty—not everybody has to be a baker. But if a few individuals decide to be bakers, they can produce enough bread for everyone. Jihad was redefined as such a vocation: if a few do it sufficiently, that caters to the needs of society, and it is not incumbent on the rest.

This doctrine, expounded by scholars on the Abbasid payroll, irritated many other scholars, who preferred the previous definition of jihad as the duty of every individual—even if the caliph himself did not call for it, it was the obligation of every Muslim to take up arms and go to the frontiers to fight. In the early Abbasid period there were Turkish warriors, recently converted to Islam, who made the long journey from Central Asia to fight on the Byzantine frontier, because this is where they could perform the duty from which the caliphs were defaulting. The aim of redefining jihad was thus to tame it. Once it was a prerogative of the caliph alone to call for jihad, he could come up with a million excuses to avoid performing it. The state could, of course, always invoke it when necessary, but most of the time the Abbasids had no intention of doing so—this was a period of thriving commerce between the Muslim world and the Byzantine Empire and India, which they did not want disrupted by every madcap saying, "I am doing jihad because these are infidels."

What about the Ghaznavid campaigns in India, then?

In some ways, they were the exceptions. Ghaznavid power, which extended over parts of eastern Iran, most of Afghanistan and into Central Asia and north-west India between 977 and 1186, was autonomous from Baghdad, though owing nominal allegiance to the Abbasid caliphs. Ethnically, the Ghaznavid state was mainly Afghan, but with a mixture of Turks, Uzbeks, and Kazakhs. At the end of the tenth and in this early eleventh centuries, its most brutal ruler, Mahmud of Ghazna (d. 1030), invaded India seventeen times, destroying and looting temples and cities in the name of jihad, leaving a legacy of animosity between Hindus and Muslims that is remembered to this day in the Indian subcontinent. But this lay beyond the sway of the Abbasids.

Would not the Crusades have revived ideas of jihad in the Middle East itself?

Indeed. The Crusades are generally viewed as military campaigns to control Jerusalem and the Holy Land between 1095 and 1291, ushering in an era of violence and warfare between European Christians and Muslims in the Middle East. But this is not the entire story. There is no doubt that the Crusades posed a major challenge to the Muslim world: we thought we were the last religion of salvation, and now Christians are invading, grabbing territory in the heart of Islam, creating a panic that Mecca itself might fall—are they going to wipe us out? But not everyone reacted in this way, and many Muslims lived with the Crusaders, made alliances with them, worshiped alongside them, and traded and exchanged goods, science, and knowledge with them.

Those who saw the Crusaders as the unequivocal enemies of Islam and the Muslims produced a radicalized religious rhetoric of exclusion and hatred. They recast jihad as once again a duty incumbent on every individual—the right to declare jihad had been appropriated by the caliphs, but the caliphs were sitting on their butts doing nothing. When Jerusalem was conquered by the Crusaders in 1099, a delegation of scholars—ironically, not from Syria or Jerusalem, but originally from Iraq—set out for Baghdad to plead with the Abbasid caliph to declare jihad and send reinforcements to reclaim Jerusalem. The tradition says that they arrived during the month of Ramadan and deliberately broke their fast in public during the daytime, a huge transgression, just to create a shock—as if they were saying that the loss of Jerusalem was much more serious than breaking one's fast intentionally. The Abbasid caliph remained completely indifferent.

The result was more and more voices arguing that we cannot depend on the rulers; fighting the infidel has to be brought back as an individual duty. In this period, more books on jihad were written than at any time before or after (until the revival of jihadism in the last few decades). These works were written by activist scholars close to rulers, of whom the most important was the Turkish sultan Nureddin of Aleppo

(d. 1174). The West knows of Saladin, the nephew of one of Nureddin's generals, but it was actually Nureddin who set up the strategy and vision that led later under Saladin to decisive defeats of the Crusaders. Jihad ideology flourished in this period, when for the first time it also began to be deployed against other Muslims—especially Shiʿis, but also deviant Sunnis. So when we get to a thinker like Ibn Taymiyya (1263–1328), a major influence on Bin Laden and modern militants like ISIS, his intransigence is not original. It reflects the energy of an intolerance toward other Muslims that emerged much earlier in the Crusader period, when scholars began to argue that it was disunity that allowed the infidels to invade. The enemy within was blamed for causing the problem, not the enemy without, and unless the internal enemy is eliminated and a religious unity is imposed, there is no chance to defeat the Crusaders. This outlook reached an unprecedented pitch once the Mongols poured into the Middle East while the Crusaders were still there, sacking Baghdad in 1258 and staging massacres in Damascus and Aleppo. They were about to take Egypt, before they were stopped in 1260 at Ain Jalut in northern Palestine by the Mamluks, an army of Turkish slaves, who were originally brought to serve in the Ayyubid armies in Syria and Egypt, but managed in 1250 to take control of state affairs and impose their rule that lasted until 1517.

For the first forty or fifty years of their history, the Mamluks were even more militantly jihad-minded than their predecessors, waging war on the Crusaders after the Mongols retreated. But once the Mongol threat had passed and they had driven out the Crusaders, the Mamluks reverted to Abbasid ways, forgetting about jihad as they started to enjoy palace life, overseeing a huge spice trade, and trading with the Italian city-states, especially Venice. Although the Mamluks ceased to have any interest in jihad, unlike the Abbasids they did not commission a group of scholars to deconstruct the way the doctrine had developed over the previous two centuries. So the last energies of jihad, dating from the Crusader period, were left within the mainstream Sunni tradition as a resource, ready to be activated, without a counter-voice. In other words, this later jihad ideology was never discredited. The Abbasids hired scholars to discredit jihad as an individual duty. The Mamluks did not. So if one goes into any seminary today, the formulation of jihad that is taught features the one that was radicalized during the Crusader period.

But did not the Ottoman state in turn have a strong ideology of jihad, with annual campaigns against the infidels along Umayyad lines?

The Ottomans picked up the culture of jihad of the Crusader period, and fought under its banner against the Byzantines for a long period lasting from 1299 until 1453 when they captured Constantinople and renamed it Istanbul. This lasted well beyond the Byzantine era and the first siege of Vienna in 1529. The Turkish term *ghazi* is synonymous with the term jihadist. Some modern Turk revisionists want to convince us that the ghazis were not actually doing jihad. That is historical nonsense, and it is shaped by the wish to invent an Ottoman past palatable to the EU so Turkey can join it. The fact that there were Christian auxiliaries in the Ottoman war machine does not mean that the Ottomans themselves were not waging jihad. Even the early Arab conquests could on occasion line up Christian forces—an Armenian army fought alongside Arabs against the Byzantines. To use groups of another faith or race as auxiliaries does not imply tolerance of that faith (we know well the use of black battalions during the US civil war and during the First and Second World Wars, yet the white society in the United States remained predominantly racist). Turkish society of that time was still tribal, a warrior society that had internalized jihad ideology. Also, the Ottomans did not introduce any development to the doctrine—they were incapable of that. Early Ottoman religious scholars felt weak, because only a few of them could master Arabic. Even when the Ottomans declared themselves caliphs in 1362, Muslims elsewhere did not take them seriously until their invasion of Syria and Egypt in 1516–1517. From that point onward, the Ottomans became the champions of Sunni Islam, and were able to entice Arab jurists to Istanbul, but they did not introduce any new changes to the jihad ideology of their predecessors. Of course, once they had to rule a huge empire, they started to settle down and jihad declined.

Their big expeditions into the Balkans—the siege of Vienna as late as 1683—were not seen as jihad?

Yes, they were. The impulse was still there, a residue of the Abode of Islam and the Abode of War. By that time, the Ottomans had turned their attention to Europe, to which they came to think they belonged, more than to Syria or Egypt. Interestingly though, in the sixteenth century the principal thrust of Ottoman jihad was against the Safavids in Iran, who represented more of a threat than a prize for them—they were not interested in conquering Iran. The Safavids were a problem because they were Shi'is and there was a large Shi'i population in eastern Anatolia, of which the Ottomans were very suspicious. The result was pre-emptive Ottoman animosity against Safavid influence in their own realm, for fear that it might cut the Ottoman Empire into two halves. They mounted many campaigns against the Shi'i Alevis, whom they called Qizilbash or "redheads," probably from an old Greek practice of wearing red hats.

3

Shiʿism and Sunnism

That raises the really big question of the division within the Muslim community (umma) between the Shiʿis and the Sunnis. How would you describe the original nature of the split? What explains the extreme savagery of the civil wars that broke out over issues of the succession, after conquests held to have been relatively mild?

When the Prophet died in 632, the issue of succession immediately arose. The tradition wants us to believe that this is when the initial split happened between Sunnis and Shiʿis. In fact, it took quite some time. Before the late eighth and early ninth centuries, one cannot really speak of Sunnism or Shiʿism. It is better to use proto-Sunnism and proto-Shiʿism to indicate the groups that developed to become later what we call Sunnis and Shiʿis. Proto-Shiʿism started as a political issue: the belief that ʿAli should have been the direct successor of

Muhammad, because he was his cousin and the husband of his daughter Fatima. Hence, the split started around political succession. However, the reasons that are generally cited ('Ali being the cousin and son-in-law of Muhammad) do not make sense. If there were groups that believed 'Ali should have been the successor, it was for other reasons. I say this because there is such a clear pattern among the first five caliphs—a pattern historians do not seem to have noticed, even though it is staring them in the eye. The first two caliphs were the fathers-in-law of the Prophet: Abu Bakr (r. 632–634) was the father of 'A'isha, and 'Umar (r. 634–644) was the father of Hafsa; both women were married to Muhammad. The third caliph, 'Uthman (r. 644–656), was married to two daughters of the Prophet—hence his nickname, Dhu al-Nurayn, which means "the one with two lights." There is much argument about whether he married them at the same time or separately, because in the Qur'an and Islamic law it is forbidden to marry two sisters at the same time. A man can marry one, divorce her, and marry the other, but not have them simultaneously. So there is a debate over whether 'Uthman was an exception to the rule, before the rule applied. Then came 'Ali (r. 656–661), who was married to Muhammad's daughter Fatima. Then we have Mu'awiya (r. 661–680), whose sister was married to the Prophet. So the first five caliphs are all related to the Prophet by marriage: each was his father-in-law, son-in-law, or brother-in-law. All of them were also first, second, or third cousins of Muhammad. How is that not a succession according to certain tribal rules of precedence?

'Ali became the fourth caliph when 'Uthman was assassinated in 656, in murky circumstances. In his short reign, he not only fought the Prophet's wife 'A'isha, but killed two of the close companions of the Prophet, Talha and Zubayr, in a battle in 656. These two were among a group of ten, the closest companions to Muhammad, who, it was believed, had been guaranteed ascent straight to Heaven as men who could do no wrong. Yet 'Ali, one of the ten, had dispatched two others. Coming after the death of 'Uthman, this posed a huge theological problem. Since they fought each other, they do not merit Paradise, which puts into doubt the legacy of Muhammad himself.

Moreover, a group of 'Ali's supporters, who came to be known as *Khawarij* (Dissenters), rebelled against him during the Battle of Siffin in 657 (which he was waging against Mu'awiya), and accused him of being an infidel who had violated the teachings of the Qur'an. Their grievance was that 'Ali agreed to give up his right to the caliphate and entered into arbitration to determine whether he or Mu'awiya should take the position. The Khawarij killed him. After 'Ali's death in 661, Mu'awiya — who had refused to acknowledge 'Ali as caliph on the grounds that the latter protected the killers of 'Uthman — was the natural choice as the brother-in-law of the Prophet, which gave him legitimacy within the community.

By the time Mu'awiya died in 680, there was no one left who was directly related to the Prophet through marriage. Mu'awiya had arranged to pass the succession to his son, Yazid. That had never been done before in Islam, and created a new institution: hereditary rule. Many people objected to it, including Husayn, the younger son of ʿAli and Fatima. When Muʿawiya became caliph, Husayn could not do anything because leadership of the movement reverted to his older brother Hasan, who was bribed by Muʿawiya not to press any claim to the caliphate. Husayn had to wait until his brother died in 670 before he could assume leadership of the movement. When Muʿawiya died and rule seemed to pass to his son Yazid, Husayn rebelled. He was convinced by a group of his father's followers to come to Kufa in southern Iraq—which indicates there was already a proto-Shiʿi community there—and stage an uprising against the Umayyads. When Yazid learnt of this, he ordered his general in Iraq to ambush and kill Husayn, whose head was brought back to Damascus and presented to him. This was no minor incident. Husayn was a grandson of the Prophet, and his killing blackened the memory of Yazid ever after.

Does that account for the strange asymmetry of the ensuing traditions—a tremendous Shiʿi account of the villainy of Muʿawiya and Yazid, and no comparable Sunni counter-attack on the legend of Husayn?

Yes, even though Yazid is a proto-Sunni figure, Sunnis do not like to talk much about him—he is a figure they want to keep out of the picture. They cannot condemn him, but they cannot easily accept him. In the Crusader period, there were attempts to cleanse his image, as a ruler who led jihad against the infidels and transmitted hadiths, preserving the Sunna of the Prophet. But earlier, the Abbasids had no interest in this. Historically, as we can see now, it was the death of Husayn which sparked the creation of Shi'ism as a religious movement that reimagined Muslim legitimacy as a sequence of imams, of whom the first was 'Ali and the third Husayn. It was the sixth imam, Ja'far al-Sadiq (d. 765), a descendant of Husayn, who seems to have shaped early Shi'ism as a belief system, even if much about this figure remains legend rather than history. Discarding the ideology of jihad, he urged withdrawal of the pious to take care of the community, and pass on knowledge of scripture.

Before he died, Sadiq declared his son Isma'il would be the next imam. But Isma'il died before his father, and Sadiq then made his other son the successor. A group of courtiers who had clustered around Isma'il, in the expectation he would be the heir, refused to accept this. They took the view that once declared the next imam, it cannot be taken back—so the son of Isma'il must now take his father's place. The result was a schism within the Shi'i community, and the birth of the Isma'ili sect, or Seveners, because they hold that Isma'il was the seventh imam. The other line of imams ended with the disappearance of the twelfth imam, for whose miraculous return Twelver Shi'is are still waiting. 'Alawis, for their part, do not believe that the twelfth imam ever existed—they stop with the Eleventh. Zaydis, who are prominent in Yemen, but also used to exist in north-western

Iran and elsewhere, do not believe that the imamate is
restricted to descendants of 'Ali and his wife Fatima. They
think *any* descendant of 'Ali can be an imam, opening up
the field to children of 'Ali whom he had with female slaves,
but hold that an imam has to prove himself on the battlefield, as well as among the community of scholars. By the
early ninth century, we have a lot of writings by Zaydi imams
which speak to the formation of a specifically Shi'i sect. By
then, Shi'ism had started to take root as a religious sect.

Did Sunnism emerge as a creed only later, in reaction?

No, it was around the same time that a proto-Sunnism
became aware of itself as a response to Shi'ism. At the
outset, Sunnism presented a chaotic scene, where every
scholar could pick up a new school of law and call it Sunni.
Tradition has it that around the year 850, the Abbasid caliph
Mutawakkil put a stop to this, determining that henceforward
just five Sunni schools and one Shi'i school of Shari'a would
be tolerated. The Shi'i school came to be named Ja'fari after
Ja'far al-Sadiq, and was codified by his followers. The five
Sunni schools were Hanafi, Shafi'i, Maliki, Hanbali, and
Zahiri. What the decision of Mutawakkil gradually meant
was that every believer must follow, and every scholar work
within, one of these schools. Many of the schools were still
quite fluid in the eighth and early ninth centuries, becoming codified only later in the ninth century. So, in terms of
law, Sunnism could be variegated. But in terms of theology,

official attempts to impose a unified system produced sharper divisions (for Sunnis, they include such schools as Ash'aris, Maturidis, Hanbalis, Mu'tazilis, and Sufis, and for Shi'is they include Zaydis, Isma'ilis, Twelvers, Nusayris, and Druzes). Quite soon Sunnis had their own version of the Prophet's life and what happened after he died, counterposed to the Shi'i version, each community projecting back onto the Prophet opinions that supported its own law and theology.

When did the majority of the Iraqi population become Shi'is? How far was the spread of Shi'ism an appropriation of Islamic doctrine by groups that were ethnically marginal in a larger state community—say, the Buyids in Iraq or the Berbers in Tunisia, who generated the Fatimids in Egypt?

No, it is a mistake to think Shi'ism appealed to marginal elements in society. Those two movements—one coming from what is today Tunisia, the other from eastern Iran—emerged in areas where the control of the central government was weakest, not because they expressed a distinct ethnic identity. Actually, after the first three or four caliphs, the military support-base of the Abbasid dynasty was largely Persian and Turkic. We know for sure the Abbasids moved their capital to Baghdad in 762 because they could not stand the energy of the 'Alids—supporters of 'Ali and his descendants—in Kufa, where proto-Sunnis were thoroughly cowed by the hostility of proto-Shi'is. The Abbasids wanted to get away and establish their own city, deciding who could reside there and who could not. That is why at the beginning Baghdad looked more like a proto-Sunni than a proto-Shi'i center. But then everybody started moving there.

The Buyids were a Shi'i dynasty, of mixed Kurdish and Daylami origin from north-western Iran. They ruled Iraq and Iran under nominal Abbasid authority in the tenth and eleventh centuries. They seem to have originally been Zaydis, but some of them were also Twelvers, and they ran the show in Iraq and Iran as Shi'i sultans under the formal aegis of a Sunni caliph. This was the first time a Shi'i dynasty had such power, and they used it to promote Shi'ism. In Aleppo, the Hamdanids were a dynasty of Twelvers, and in Egypt the ruling house of Fatimids was Isma'ili. So in the mid tenth century, the central parts of the Muslim world were ruled by Shi'is. Just as centuries earlier many people became Muslims out of convenience, so now many became Shi'is. Rural Syria would remain predominantly Shi'i until the arrival of the Ottomans. In the fifteenth and sixteenth centuries, some prestigious Shi'i scholars from south Lebanon moved to Iran, increasing the intellectual weight of the Shi'i population there.

The same state pressures worked the other way round when Sunni rulers had the upper hand. The coast of what is today Lebanon was inhabited by either Shi'is or Christians, but when the Mamluks arrived in the late thirteenth century with their war machine they forced all Shi'is—Twelvers, Isma'ilis, or Druzes—back into the mountains and sometimes up into the Bekaa Valley, and imported Turkic and

Kurdish tribes to settle the areas they had cleansed. The Ottomans continued such policies on a large scale, intimidating many Shi'is into converting to Sunnism. That is why if we look at the topography of Syria today, we find all these small Shi'i villages around Aleppo, which was predominantly Shi'i until a series of Sunni rulers—Nureddin, Saladin, then the Mamluks, and the Ottomans—changed the composition of the city, where people either converted or left for a few surrounding villages.

In the same way, contemporary Iran is now majority Shi'i, but that is a result of the similar policies pursued by the Safavids starting in the late fifteenth century, intimidating Sunnis into either converting or leaving. For a long period, southern Iraq was also under Safavid control, and because it contained the holiest Shi'i shrines there was a lot of deliberate population movement there, to cater for the pilgrimages to them. That explains why southern Iraq is predominantly Shi'i, whereas northern Iraq—for a long time under Ottoman control—is Sunni; and also why the Kurds in Iran are not Sunni but Shi'i, whereas in northern Iraq and Turkey they are predominantly Sunnis.

The 'Alawi community in Syria has no connection with the period of Hamdanid power—their version of Shi'ism is quite distinctive?

There are two Shi'i communities whose theology ruffles mainstream Twelver Shi'is, let alone Sunnis. The 'Alawis, who are also called Nusayris, believe that 'Ali was meant to be God's prophet, but the angel Gabriel became confused and went to Muhammad instead—and that when 'Ali died, he was borne up to heaven and waits there to return on the Day of Judgment. There are also the Druzes, whose religion blends elements all the way from Buddhism to ancient Greek philosophy. The Druzes consider Plato and John the Baptist as prophets—John's shrine in the Great Mosque of Damascus is mainly visited by Druzes. Vehemently denounced by Sunni scholars, both communities were pushed into the mountainous western areas of greater Syria and south-eastern Anatolia.

What are the historical differences between the Alevis of Turkey and the 'Alawis of Syria? Is the common nomenclature just a confusion?

The only thing the two groups share is that both are Shi'is. But they are ethnically distinct and their beliefs are not the same. The name *Alevi* was the Ottoman term for Shi'is in general, because of their reverence for 'Ali as the first imam, and *'Alawi* was its version in Arabic. Both groups exist in Turkey today, though in very unequal proportions. The 'Alawis are an Arab—or Arabic-speaking—community spread along the upper coast of the eastern Mediterranean, from northern Lebanon to the province of Hatay in Turkey, once Alexandretta in French-ruled Syria. There are two to three million of them in Syria, with maybe another half million in Turkey and Lebanon. Traditionally, they were known in Islam as Nusayris. They believe in eleven, rather than twelve, imams and their religion incorporates a collage of Islamic and non-Islamic doctrines. Historically, Sunnis regarded them as heretical, as some Sunnis still do today. Most of the Alevis, on the other hand, are ethnically Turkic, descending from tribes that once occupied parts of what are now eastern Anatolia, Azerbaijan, and north-eastern Iran. Today they exist as such only in Turkey, where they number perhaps ten million—there is no accurate count of them. They share the Twelver version of Shi'ism that dominates Iran, but in forms heavily infused by a mystical outlook.

Alevi practices today seem quite distant from Iranian Shi'ism. Mosques are less important, prayers are much fewer, women do not have to cover their heads. How did they stray so far?

We see the same pattern among the Druzes in Lebanon. A belief system may start as part of a larger movement, but if a group that holds it in common becomes isolated, it will tend to develop distinctive features protective of its identity— much like a language, which if it is removed from its original matrix, will develop differently, sometimes retaining primitive strands that have disappeared elsewhere. The Alevis lived under the wing of the Ottomans for almost 500 years, in conditions where the retention (or invention) of specific beliefs, rituals, or dress helped them to resist absorption by the dominant community and preserve their own identity.

Could it be said that persecution of the Alevis in Anatolia started earlier, and has perhaps been more continuous, than that of any other significant Shi'i community in the Middle East, with successive waves of repression by the Ottomans, by Kemal Ataturk, and now by Erdoğan? If so, what would explain their treatment?

Both groups—Alevis and 'Alawis—were persecuted, but for different reasons. The 'Alawis were persecuted by Sunni rulers because they inhabited coastal areas, and during the medieval period were viewed as a fifth column who collab-orated with the Crusaders (though one has to say that many Sunnis worked with the Crusaders as well). The Mamluks and Ottomans would send special military campaigns to destroy 'Alawi villages, and as a matter of policy encour-aged Turkic and Kurdish tribes to settle in 'Alawi areas. The Alevis, by contrast, were persecuted from the late fifteenth century onwards because the Ottomans saw them as poten-tial agents and allies of Safavid Iran, their greatest enemy in the east. Historically, it was Alevi tribes that helped the Safavid dynasty attain power in Iran. In the wars between the Ottomans and the Safavids, the Alevis occupied villages and towns straddling the border between the two empires, and the Safavids naturally tried to use them in order to expand into Anatolia. The Ottomans therefore initiated pol-icies of persecution and marginalization of the Alevis that were visited and revisited throughout Ottoman history and modern Turkey. Kemal Ataturk's motives sprang from his push for Turkish nationalism, which hit out at all ethnic or religious minorities (be they Armenians, Kurds, Alevis, ʿAlawis, even Sunni mystics or Dervish orders, as they were called in Turkish) that in his view stood in the face of his particular brand of reform and change.

The memory of this history is reawakened today amid the conflicts between Sunnis and Shiʿis in the Middle East, but overlaid with another layer of problems unique to Turkey. On the one hand, Turkey is opposed to Iran, because Tehran supports the Assad regime in Syria that Erdoğan wants to bring down, and he suspects it of meddling in Turkish affairs by reaching out to ʿAlawis and Alevis as fellow Shiʿis. On the other hand, Erdoğan and his party are pushing for a transformation of the Turkish political system, with a discourse stressing that Turkey is first and foremost a country for Turks—that is, orthodox Sunni Turks who should answer to him and no one else. So groups that have traditionally been marginalized and persecuted, especially Alevis, ʿAlawis, Kurds, and Armenians, offer Erdoğan an opportunity to remind Turks that these have always been the inherent enemies of a strong Turkey—even though in the case of the Kurds, they are Sunnis.

What explains the apparent paradox in the respective positions of the Shiʿi communities in Syria and Iraq? In Syria, the ʿAlawi are a minority of at most 15 percent of the population, yet have ruled the country under the Assad clan for close to fifty years, while in Iraq the Shiʿis form a majority of the Arab

*population and a plurality in the country as a whole, yet only
achieved power by grace of the American occupation in the
last few years?*

There is a logic to this. In Syria the 'Alawis were driven
into the mountainous regions of the coast, which became
their historic homeland where they could find refuge from
Sunni domination of the cities on the plains. In the early
twentieth century, they remained marginalized under the
French and during the first decade of Syrian independence,
when a Sunni establishment of merchants and politicians
ran the new state, interspersed with a few coups reflecting
the power struggles within this Syrian Sunni establishment.
The 'Alawis had no big banks, they owned no big businesses,
they did not control the bazaars in Damascus or Aleppo:
they served as lowly foot-soldiers in the Sunni economic
machine. How could they improve their position? They had
two possible routes. One bloc of 'Alawis started to put their
bets on the pan-Syrian—inter-confessional—projects of the
Baath Party, as an avenue of upward political mobility. But
as in many other countries of the Middle East, the primary
way disenfranchised or historically persecuted groups could
hope to improve their position was to enter the army. So the
'Alawis also gravitated toward the military, where promotion
through the ranks promised an escape from their inferior
condition. Thus when the Baath Party came to power in
Syria in the 1960s, the 'Alawis were well placed to take
advantage of the change. They were embedded in the party,

and they had a lot of key players in the army. After elimi-
nating rivals or enemies within his own community, Hafez
Assad—Minster of Defense at the time—could engineer an
'Alawi take-over of Syria, at the head of a group of fellow
officers and some politicians. There his family and community remain in power today.

In Iraq, the same kind of dynamic was at work, but in the
opposite direction. There the Shi'is were the Arab majority, outnumbering Sunnis. Under the Hashemite monarchy
the British installed in Iraq, the Shi'is controlled most of
the economic landscape. Thus, they were not driven by a
desperate push for empowerment. The Sunnis in Iraq, on
the other hand, had never benefited much from Ottoman
rule in a society split by ethnicity as well as confession, with
a large Kurdish population. The Arab Sunnis in Iraq were
a minority. After the Second World War, they too enrolled
in the Baath party and joined the army in pursuit of power,
which they seized about the same time as the 'Alawis did
in Syria. The pattern was essentially comparable, but with
opposite sectarian outcomes. That is what largely explains
the hatred the Baathists in Iraq and in Syria felt toward each
other, although their ideology and even their party were
technically the same.

4

Salafism and Militant Islam

Rigorist forms of Sunnism are now typically termed Salafi. How recent is the general currency of this term, and what are its origins?

The term *Salafi*, which indicates attachment to the predecessors, has always been there. Some applied it narrowly, some applied it broadly. In the Middle Ages, when people used the term *salaf*, they meant the predecessors who, generally speaking, lived in the first two centuries of Islam. The salaf included the Prophet Muhammad, his companions and their companions, and over the years came to include as well a few notable scholars. It is a classic designation evoking the envy later Muslims felt toward the earliest Muslim generations who had had the privilege of accompanying and learning from Muhammad and from his companions. More importantly, the salaf came to be revered for their crucial contribution to the formation of Islam. This was the kind of respect in which, say, the Founding Fathers in the United States are held. Americans idealize them in some ways even though it is well known that they were racists, owned slaves, and committed many other indecencies, but they passed to us some lessons by which we try to live, not a Golden Age we have to imitate blindly and recreate. In the eighteenth and nineteenth centuries, there developed in the Muslim world several movements with conceptions more like those of the Renaissance in Europe—that there had been a Dark Age which is responsible for the state of weakness and ignorance, and to emerge from it we must recover the light of Islam's golden age, that of the salaf. So, in contemporary usage, a Salafi means someone who wants as literally as possible to model their faith and lifestyle on the example of the glorious predecessors. Salafis believe these predecessors copied the purest form of Islam—word for word—from the Prophet Muhammad.

Historically, this is utter nonsense. But history is beside the point here. Modern Salafism does have some medieval roots, which we find in Ibn Taymiyya and his celebrated student Ibn Qayyim al-Jawziyya (d. 1350), two of the smartest and most fanatical scholars Islam ever produced. Most Salafis belong to the Hanbali school, an activist strand of Islam with some similarities to Puritanism. Hanbali scholars were the religious bullies of their societies, leading street gangs that often took the law into their own hands. In the tenth century, there is a famous example of Hanbali mobs besieging one of Islam's most celebrated historians, Tabari (d. 922), in his house for weeks on end, because they objected to his views about their founder Ahmad ibn Hanbal. Also, Ibn Taymiyya formed a gang to patrol the neighborhoods of Damascus and destroy shrines and edifices that he considered unorthodox. So there are some medieval traces of what would become features of later Salafism.

The modern forms of Salafism really started in the eighteenth and nineteenth centuries. One strand was rather liberal, and was initially advocated by two moderate thinkers: Jamal al-Din al-Afghani (d. 1897) and Muhammad ʿAbduh (d. 1905) who was grand mufti of Egypt between 1899 and 1905. Their idea was to create an Islamic renaissance by looking at the way the predecessors in the Golden Age (roughly the first four centuries of Islam) did it. They were not imitative, although they placed most of the blame on what they called "non-Islamic" ideas and trends that crept into Islam and corrupted the Muslims (Shiʿism, Sufism, etc.). This form of Salafism, despite its early popularity, is almost non-existent today.

Radical Salafism, however, is imitative, and is tied on the one hand to Wahhabism and on the other hand to an influential Islamic thinker named Rashid Rida (d. 1935), who was born in Lebanon but moved to Egypt in his early thirties. Rida began as a pupil of Muhammad ʿAbduh and developed some of his teacher's views in a very fundamentalist way. Rida believed that the class of religious scholars had become corrupt (in terms of their blind adherence to

innovations and complacency with political rulers), and
that Islamic renewal is a collective duty: if the Muslims do
not pursue it, they all sin. In his view, Muslims must seek
to reestablish the Islamic state and live according to the
original Shari'a of the Salaf, which was based on the teachings of Muhammad and the Qur'an. He also called for the
revival of the Arabic language as the language of Islam. So,
whereas 'Abduh had accommodated a lot of reform based on
a modern political philosophy that takes into account what
is best for Muslims today, Rida insisted that whenever there
is a clear text (in the Sunna of Muhammad or the Qur'an)
it must be followed. In this respect, he came closer to the
narrow-minded Wahhabism, which insisted that Muslims
must observe Islam exactly the way the Prophet Muhammad
defined it and his companions applied it.

Rida expounded his views in his influential newspaper
al-Manar (the Lighthouse), and also developed them in a
powerful interpretation of the Qur'an, *Tafsir al-Manar*. The
British did not interfere with him—he seems, in fact, to
have been on quite good terms with them. What they were
wary of was pan-Arabism. They were quite tolerant of pan-
Islamism, which they hoped would counteract pan-Arabism.
In that they were not wrong: for a long time, pan-Arabism
and pan-Islamism rarely saw eye to eye on anything in the
Middle East. It was really only after the Second World War
that Muslims generally started to think of Salafism in the
way that Rida and Wahhabism, rather than Afghani and
'Abduh, understood it.

But the conversion of Salafism into a widespread currency —used pretty much everywhere as an "-ism" in the modern sense, standing for the most dissatisfied form of contemporary Islam—is much more recent (since the 1980s), and has been quite sudden. It has a lot to do with political problems in the Muslim world and Saudi sponsorship of Wahhabism. Salafis today try to relive *precisely* how they imagine the Prophet Muhammad, his companions, and a very few others once lived. These predecessors created the ideal Islamic community, which it is the duty of Muslims to recreate here and now. Muslims who do not adhere to this model are errant followers of innovations that have no religious legitimacy. As in any other movement, Salafi ideologues disagree on minor points, mainly relating to how they can most effectively achieve their goals, much like different kinds of Marxists vying over the best route to their promised land.

How specific is the Wahhabism that emerged in the Arabian Peninsula in the eighteenth century as a doctrine and movement, within the broader phenomenon of Salafism?

The eighteenth century witnessed the rise of several movements of religious reform, of which the Wahhabi movement was just one, if the most notorious and most successful. Its founder, Ibn 'Abd-ul-Wahhab (d. 1792), contended that return to the practices of the Salaf was not enough. Muslims had become so corrupt that they must undertake a *hijra* (immigration) as the early followers of Muhammad were required to do, cutting their ties with polytheistic Arabian society and joining him in Medina. Ibn ʿAbd-ul-Wahhab mandated the same disconnection: Muslims must cut themselves off from their society and its heretical practices, not only spiritually but physically, abandoning their tribes and rallying to him in the small oasis of Dirʿiyya in Najd (central Arabia), where he had formed an alliance with the local clan chief Muhammad ibn Saʿud (d. 1765) and after that his son ʿAbd-ul-ʿAziz Ibn Saʿud (d. 1803). This was a radical innovation. It was no longer sufficient to look back at how Muslims at the time of the Prophet lived, like most traditional Salafis would do. The duty of the faithful was to recreate the ideal Islam anew, and that required re-initiation into Islam by joining the religious leader and receiving his indoctrination—not unlike the baptism Protestants must undergo if they convert to Catholicism because the Protestant baptism is void. Most of these followers were single men of fighting age. Sociologically, if you break up tribal identities in this fashion, you create a tremendous potential for aggressive energy—young males who are not going to sit around drinking tea and eating cake all day. So a dynamic was unleashed like that of the original Arab expansion when Islam destabilized the old tribal relations, coalescing around the new faith a mass of single men whose tensions were released in the conquests.

In Najd, ʿAbd-ul-ʿAziz Ibn Saʿud was not yet a dominant player. He had his own ambitions, and saw in a pact with Ibn ʿAbd-ul-Wahhab, who was no warrior but whose propaganda helped consolidate Ibn Sa'ud's power in Najd, a way to acquire more manpower. The House of Sa'ud has always tended to think of the Wahhabis as foot-soldiers they could use for their political ends and dispense with when they were no longer needed, but that is not how the relationship would always work out. Toward the end of the eighteenth century, Wahhabi forces started to fan out in raids beyond Najd. Their wrath was first directed at Shi'is—in a few days' ride from Najd, they could be at the door of small cities in lower Iraq, suddenly materializing out of the desert to surprise these communities. In larger numbers, Wahhabi militants led by Ibn Sa'ud stormed out of the Arabian Peninsula in 1801 and 1802, desecrating and destroying the holiest Shi'i religious sites in Kerbala and Najaf (including the shrine of imam Husayn), and killing thousands of Shi'is. Next, they launched a series of attacks against Mecca and Medina, occupying them in 1804–1805. Since Wahhabi doctrine held any form of tomb visitation to be apostasy, in Medina they demolished several tombs, including that of Prophet Muhammad himself. Then they attacked Jordan and southern Syria, perpetrating widespread massacres of Shi'is, Christians, and Druzes, and panick-ing many others into flight to Palestine and to Lebanon, to Damascus and northern parts of Syria. There are chilling similarities between what happened then and what ISIS does today.

*What explains the timing of the sudden emergence and dyna-
mism of the Wahhabi movement in Arabia in the eighteenth
century?*

Most scholars now think that movements of religious reform
—liberal or fanatical—can be found virtually everywhere at
that time in the Muslim world. There was a troubled mood
and many—especially those with some education—were
losing confidence in their society, and starting to ask: where
are we going, are we on the right track? The West did not yet
control large parts of the Muslim world, but it was already
making encroachments. Ibn ʿAbd-ul-Wahhab was no stellar
student, but he had to go to southern Iraq to get his religious
education, and there he became aware of what was hap-
pening in India and Iran, where European imperialism was
starting to make an impact. In the Arab world, the Ottomans
were visibly starting to weaken, exacerbating this sense of
anxiety. This was a time when Ottoman rulers were completely focused on the European scene: the Arabian, Yemeni,
even Egyptian parts of their empire had become a back-
drop for the ruling elite in Istanbul, to which they did not
pay much attention. For Ibn ʿAbd-ul-Wahhab, and not him
alone, this meant the leaders of Sunni Islam were not doing
their job—they were failing to protect Muslims and to guard
the House of Islam. So in this vacuum, all kinds of apocalyptic, messianic, and militant movements began to bubble up
in what are today Libya, Egypt, Nigeria, even in India, where
Shah Wali Allah (d. 1762) was another important reformer.

So to what extent was Wahhabism originally aimed as much against Ottoman as against Shi'i presence in the region?

The Wahhabis were opposed to all Muslims who differed from them. Ibn 'Abd-ul-Wahhab preached against every form of Islamic "corruption," which meant anything that did not meet his approval—religious, social, or political. He saw no separation between politics and religion. That is why in his opinion it was essential that the politician and the jurist team up together to make sure that the state enforces and propagates the teachings of the true religion. This was also the only way the House of Sa'ud could secure its own legitimacy and the loyalty of the Wahhabis. The Ottomans lacked any ability to suppress the threat of Wahhabism directly, so they appealed to their nominal viceroy in Egypt, the great Muhammad 'Ali (d. 1849), who originally came from Albania and established a dynasty that ruled Egypt (and at times Sudan) until the overthrow of the monarchy in 1952, to deal with them. Muhammad 'Ali sent several expeditions into Arabia between 1811 and 1818, ultimately crushing the Wahhabis and capturing their political leader, 'Abdullah Ibn Sa'ud, the grandson of 'Abd-ul-'Aziz. Ibn Sa'ud was sent to Istanbul and executed by the Ottomans in 1818. This, of course, proved only a temporary solution, and Wahhabism would reemerge in force again in the twentieth century.

Ibn 'Abd-ul-Wahhab died shortly before Napoleon invaded Egypt, but 'Abd-ul-'Aziz was attacking Iraq while the French were still in occupation of the Nile. Did the arrival of the French play any role in Wahhabi expansion?

The fact that the French got to Egypt and Napoleon tried to march along the coast up to Syria without the Ottomans being able to do anything about it was a green light for Ibn Saʿud. Demonstrating how weak the Ottomans had become, it meant he now had a chance to consolidate his power beyond Najd. He jumped at the opportunity, and after occupying Mecca and Medina, marched north. Today we think of Jordan as a country, but geographically speaking, it is just an extension of northern parts of the Najd. Growing up in Lebanon, I could still come across old people whose grandparents spoke of surviving as children the early nineteenth-century Wahhabi attack. The desert that extends north from Najd takes you all the way to Daraa, just south of Damascus, an area that in the early nineteenth century was mainly inhabited by Druzes and Christians. After the Wahhabis slaughtered them or forced them to flee, other Sunnis came in to live in the vacant villages—in lots of places, Sunni settlement is relatively recent. As for Muhammad ʿAli, after bailing out the Ottomans for years—even sending a huge Egyptian army to Greece to try, unsuccessfully, to put down the Greek rebellion there that resulted in Greek independence—he thought, why not take over the Ottoman Empire itself? In the 1840s, his army marched all the way to southern Anatolia, and it took the combined European powers to stop him.

Did the teachings of Ibn ʿAbd-ul-Wahhab leave a significant imprint on Salafism outside the Arabian Peninsula, after the crushing of the movement by Muhammad ʿAli? For example, was Rida affected by them?

A little. He was never a Wahhabi, but knew about them. In his last phase, by the 1920s, he came closer to some of the ideas of Ibn ʿAbd-ul-Wahhab, realizing how much he had in common with Wahhabism, but he did not make a complete jump. At that time, the Wahhabi movement had no capabilities outside of Saudi Arabia, and did not really appeal to anyone else. By the early twentieth century, many Muslims were saying, we need to go back and relearn Islam as the Salaf practiced it. But most of those conversations were academic in character, confined to intellectuals, and known only in small learned circles. They did not translate into mass movements. These intellectual eddies are extremely interesting as historical phenomena, but they did not become major trends on the street. That is why, when Wahhabism took off in recent years, it seemed very much like a comet that attracts all the dust and all the small objects in space that lie in its path, because it has such pulling force as a movement that promises to turn theory into actuality. At that point, lots of Salafis came under the spell of Wahhabism, even if they had tactical disagreements with it or minor theological divergences.

How far is the modern importance of Wahhabism simply a
product of its original attachment to the Sa'ud clan in Najd,
and the accidental wealth and power the dynasty later acquired
from oil, bankrolling its institutional diffusion throughout the
Muslim world in very recent times? Or did it possess an unu-
sually strong proselytizing impulse from the start?

The agreement that Ibn 'Abd-ul-Wahhab had with
Muhammad ibn Sa'ud—the founder of the House of
Sa'ud—was in some ways a stroke of genius that assured the
success of each of them. The irony is that each of the two
thought he was getting the better deal. To this day, some
members of the Saudi royal family think they control the
Wahhabis and benefit from them but can put an end to
them if and when they wish, while the Wahhabis think they
determine whether or not the royal family stays in power.
Of course, things are not quite as simple as this, since some
members of the royal family are committed Wahhabi fanatics.
Over the years, the two camps have become like conjoined
twins: one cannot function without the other. Without their
attachment to the House of Sa'ud in the Najd, Ibn 'Abd-ul-
Wahhab and his followers would not have had any chance of
success, just as the modern spread of Wahhabism would not
have been possible without the unconditional sponsorship of
the Saudi royal family and Saudi state.

Fortune certainly smiled on the House of Sa'ud. In
the 1920s, British imperial interests, which had originally
backed their Hashemite rivals in Arabia, temporarily moved

to the side of the Sa'ud clan as a fire-break against what were seen as the dangers of pan-Arabism. Though there was never unanimity in London—H. St.J.B. Philby (d. 1960) was sponsoring Ibn Sa'ud, while J.B. Glubb (d. 1986) was working for Faisal—Britain effectively helped the Kingdom of Saudi Arabia into being. The Wahhabis were back, and, with the discovery of large deposits of oil in the Kingdom in 1938, far richer than ever before. God was on their side. In due course, they found a still more powerful patron in the United States.

From the outset, long before petroleum, Wahhabism was a movement centrally focused on proselytizing. Its ideology was so foreign, and even offensive, to mainstream Islam that for over a century it had very little appeal to Muslims outside the perimeter of the House of Sa'ud. It was not until the coffers of the Kingdom were flush with money that Wahhabism found a large audience willing to listen to it. Once it was empowered with cash, it could essentially buy its way into the hearts and minds of Muslims. Hence the spread of Wahhabism into Pakistan, Egypt, Syria, Jordan, Lebanon, the Caucasus, Turkey, Africa, Western Europe, and even the US. Scholars coming out of seminaries with no prospect of work anywhere were now attracted by Wahhabi money. The Saudis also set up religious seminaries for Wahhabi instruction, which attracted many students who had no chance of getting to a university in their own countries, much as others once went to Soviet Russia. For their part, keen to attract aid and investment from the Saudi rulers, Muslim

countries themselves diametrically opposed to the ideology of Wahhabism opened their doors to its propagandists,
giving it access to large swathes of their subjects. The rulers
of these countries thought of Wahhabi preachers as a bunch
of crazies whom they could eliminate whenever an opportune moment arose.

What would be examples?

Take Jordan, where if people in the south—especially in the
city of Maʿan—had their way, they would join Saudi Arabia
because of the power of Salafi ideologues there. But since
the Jordanian state is dependent on handouts from Saudi
Arabia, the Hashemite monarchy cannot simply repress the
Salafis. They keep them under scrutiny, to make sure that
they cannot get to the point where they become a direct
threat; but the Jordanians also know they cannot go too far.
Another case would be Lebanon, where the billionaire construction magnate Rafik Hariri (d. 2005) was brought back to
the country by the Saudis to become prime minister, at the
price of allowing Salafis to come to Sunni towns and cities to
preach. Because the Saudis were behind his political adven-
ture in Lebanon, he had to turn a blind eye to what Salafi
propagandists were up to. Gradually they gained momentum, to a point where nowadays his son Saad does not control
the Sunnis in Lebanon the way his father used to do. If you
look at Sunnis in Lebanon today, many are under the spell of
Salafism, and many others hate Hariri for empowering them.

*When you say that Wahhabi ideology is so offensive to main-
stream Islam, what are the key points that cause most offense?*

At the heart of Sunni Islam, there is what you might call the
idea of compromise—the belief that no one sect has it completely right. Sunni religious scholars had to allow for the
possibility that they could be wrong, and other Sunni scholars
could get it right. They not only had to respect the diversity
of views, but when they spoke of religion, they reflected that
diversity in their own thought and works. In offering their
opinions, they accommodated others as also valid. If one
looks at mainstream Sunni scholarship—and to be honest,
I only became aware of this later through research, I did not
see it at the beginning—whether books of theology, interpretations of the Qur'an, or collections of hadiths, what one
realizes is that they end up contradicting each other. There
was a famous thirteenth-century Damascene hadith scholar
called Nawawi (d.1278), who composed a popular small collection of forty hadiths by the Prophet Muhammad. If we
read this at a sitting, it is utterly confusing. What is Islam?
One hadith says it means performing some rituals (which he
defines differently in different hadiths); another hadith tells
you it is to honor your parents. What is more important: To
be sincere and treat people well or to believe in God? Is it
critical to avoid sinning, or does it not really matter whether
you sin or not, since God will forgive you even if you have
tons of sins on your conscience? I am not talking about a
collection of 400 or 4,000 hadiths; this is just forty of them.

Nawawi had to accommodate the fact that the Sunnis do not agree on all of these things.

That is what classical Sunni Islam was like. Because there was no imam to lead all the Sunnis, it was much like academia today—you can bring different people together to talk about Lincoln, Shakespeare, or any other topic, and four speakers on a panel can completely disagree with each other, and at the end of the day go to a pub for a drink together; and if they write about it, they will say this was my opinion, but others saw things differently. That is essentially what we call mainstream Sunni Islam. Of course, when it comes to Shiʿis, no, they are not part of the conversation—Sunnis consider them rejectionists (*rafida*), the popular Sunni term for them, or if extreme, heretics. But, among Sunnis themselves there was acceptance of diversity, and if anybody started to say other Sunnis were not good Muslims, they would close ranks against them. In the eighteenth and nineteenth centuries, even among scholars we can more or less classify as Salafi, none ever shared the brutal Wahhabi insistence that the problem lies with the Muslims who, if they do not join Wahhabism, are not Muslims, and are not only to be punished, but a jihad must be launched against them. Such language had never before been used in Islamic history. When Ibn ʿAbd-ul-Wahhab even declared all other Sunnis heretics because they practiced Islam the wrong way, visiting tombs and making vows, venerating saints or lapsing into mysticism, his was a doctrine deeply alien to mainstream Sunnis at the time, or as they were throughout Islamic history.

Is not that too homogeneous an image of classical Sunnism? How would such a leading figure as Ibn Taymiyya fit into it? Or was it just that Ibn 'Abd-ul-Wahhab had charisma as a preacher, whereas Ibn Taymiyya had only authority as a scholar?

There was a difference. Ibn 'Abd-ul-Wahhab was a very charismatic preacher, whereas Ibn Taymiyya was a charismatic person but was essentially a scholar, whose audience was quite restricted. For Sunnis had divided into sub-sects, and Ibn Taymiyya had authority only among the Hanbalis in Damascus, and a very few other individuals. By default his prowess as a preacher did not become a magnet, since his audience was inherently limited. On the one hand, there was an audience that was going to listen to him, irrespective of how eloquent or otherwise he was, because they were Hanbalis; on the other hand, he had no access to other sects because they would not go to a mosque where he was teaching—they went to hear their own preachers. Ibn 'Abd-ul-Wahhab was not much of a scholar, probably a C-grade student; his writings are not particularly intelligent. Ibn Taymiyya was of an altogether different stature. The reason why after his death even people who did not agree with him would read his writings is that they were impressed by the vastness of his knowledge. Over time people started to forget how his views came to be built. Ibn Taymiyya's simplified doctrine is that if something does not have strong support in the Qur'an or the Sunna of Muhammad, then we cannot say it is Islamic. Even if it seems morally valuable or socially valid, still it is not Islamic. So he rejected many practices as un-Islamic. Nevertheless, his means of giving force to his words was limited. He had a gang who would do his bidding in Damascus, but there were other gangs, and in the last analysis there was a ruler with the power of the law, and when Ibn Taymiyya crossed a line, he was arrested and put in jail—he went to prison five times. Once he was thrown into jail for a year before he was even given an audience before the sultan to defend himself. There was a strong power in Syria at the time to put a check on him. There was no such power to check Ibn 'Abd-ul-Wahhab in Najd—on the contrary, Saudi power enabled and promoted his preaching.

There was a second difference. Ibn Taymiyya was functioning in Damascus where there were other powerful scholars who could stand up to him and tell him to his face, you are wrong, we do not agree with you, and who could make sense to an audience, drawing it to them instead. In Arabia at the time of Ibn 'Abd-ul-Wahhab, there were no established scholars in Najd. At the most, there might be something like a village curate, who barely knew how to read. Ibn 'Abd-ul-Wahhab faced no competition whatsoever. Any serious scholar who had studied in the seminaries of Iraq would not land up in Najd, which was an intellectual wilderness. He would go to a place like Mecca or Medina, or some major city like Damascus or Cairo, or if aiming at the most prestigious positions in scholarship, would stay in Iraq. The fact

that he returned to Najd meant that nobody thought of him
as particularly gifted.

*In the case of Ibn Taymiyya, how significant was the recent
history of the Crusades as a formative context for his thought?*

For a long time the standard view was that Ibn Taymiyya's
preaching was mostly just rhetoric. There is a tendency to
praise him as a thinker and suggest that it was the threat from
the Mongols that really shaped his outlook, other concerns
being essentially secondary or insignificant. I think this is an
exaggeration. There is a false impression that the Crusades
came to an end in 1292 when the Crusades were kicked
out by the Mamluks, and since most of what Ibn Taymiyya
wrote was produced after that, there cannot be a connection
between the two. In reality, the Crusaders remained a serious
threat well into the middle of the fourteenth century—in
1327 they sacked and burnt Alexandria and were still con-
stantly raiding the shores of the eastern Mediterranean. For
anyone living in Damascus, these attacks were all too present
a danger. Ibn Taymiyya himself—this is a little-known
episode, about which I have recently written—was directly
involved in a delegation sent to ensure that the Shi'is and
Druzes of Mount Lebanon stopped cooperating with the
Crusaders. The *fatwas* he wrote make it very clear that what
he feared was not these communities themselves, but their
potential collaboration with the Crusaders, with whom they
had worked in the past. The options he listed for dealing

with these Muslim "heretics" were: kill them, burn their villages to drive them out of the area, or force them to convert to Sunnism. There is no room for a political settlement in his outlook. The wound of the Crusades was still very, very fresh. The Mongols too, of course, were a huge danger. Under threat from the east and from the west, the survival of Sunni Islam was at stake. To understand Ibn Taymiyya's thinking, this is the context to keep in mind.

What explains the virulent recrudescence of antagonisms between Sunnis and Shi'is in the Middle East today? Tensions on this scale between the two communities have not existed for many centuries. What is the contemporary dynamic behind them?

There are three major figures of modern Islam who were pan-Islamists: Qutb (1906–1966) in Egypt; Khomeini (1902–1989) in Iran; and Mawdudi (1903–1979) in India–Pakistan. All three wanted Muslims to transcend their differences, in an Islamic unity capable of triumphing over the twin evils of decadent capitalism and atheistic communism. For each, Muslims were living in a time—there were eschatological overtones—when believers were being squeezed between these two rocks, forced to opt for one or the other. They pitched Islam as an alternative, but only on the condition that Muslims could unite. In the Sunni world, Mawdudi and Qutb preached pan-Islamism, but both of them died before their ideas gained any wide audience. It was the success of the Iranian Revolution in 1979 that transformed the ideological landscape. Khomeini's original project was a grandiose pan-Islamism, uniting Shi'is and Sunnis alike in a common battle against the two enemies of all Muslims: the USA and USSR. But once Saddam Hussein launched his attack on Iran, threatening the survival of the Islamic Republic, Khomeini was forced onto the defensive, and had to compromise his vision. Under siege at home, the unity of all believers lay out of reach. What could be achieved, however, was pan-Shi'ism. The Iranian regime opened up lines of communication to Shi'is everywhere, sending them support—including arms, money, expertise—without any conditions. Wherever there were Shi'is of any kind—in Yemen, in Syria, in Lebanon, in Iraq, in Bahrain—there was a tremendous flow of advice and assistance. Never before under any Shi'i dynasty had there been this level of tolerance to all forms of Shi'ism. In the past, there had always been pressure for conversion: you should become a Twelver. Khomeinism avoided that. Zaydis, 'Alawis, Druzes could remain who they were, without aggressive theological instructions from Iran. All that was necessary was Shi'i solidarity. The strategy was designed to create regional support for the Iranian Revolution, which felt itself the object of Western aggression—this is a recurrent theme in modern Iranian history, from the constitutional movement of 1908–1911 to the overthrow of Mosaddegh in 1953 and onwards. The success story of Khomeini's policy was the emergence of Hezbollah as the most powerful force in Lebanon after 1982.

The second transformative event was the Soviet invasion of Afghanistan, also in 1979. That gave perfect momentum to a pan-Islamism from the other direction, a Sunni variant. The Afghan success in driving the Red Army out of the country had an ideological impact comparable to that of the overthrow of the Shah. The Iranians showed they could defeat the West, and the Sunnis had now defeated the East: Islam can triumph over both capitalism and communism. But just as Khomeini's pan-Islamism was forced back into a pan-Shi'ism by the Iran–Iraq war, so Sunni pan-Islamism contracted, under the pressure of the same war, into a pan-Sunnism. Saddam Hussein himself, who started out as an extremely secular leader, switched over and launched religious rhetoric to appeal for Sunni assistance once he looked like losing the war, pitching himself as a champion of Sunnism even though the majority of Iraqis were Shi'is. Then came the Gulf War (1990–1991) and the 2003 American invasion of Iraq, which split the Sunni and Shi'i communities in the country wider apart than they had ever been in the past, cementing the hostility between pan-Shi'ism and pan-Sunnism in the Middle East today.

To what extent does contemporary pan-Sunnism derive from the ideas of Qutb or Mawdudi?

The ideas of Mawdudi and Qutb figure to some extent in the sense that both are widely read among pan-Islamist activists, especially Sunnis. The irony is that pan-Sunnism is now a

Salafi pan-Sunnism—principally the Wahhabi variant proclaimed by the Saudi monarchy and some offshoots of it who do not anymore answer to Saudi Arabia (notably al-Qaeda and ISIS)—which has sunk roots everywhere in the Sunni world. Saudi Arabia, and to a lesser extent Qatar, stand as the champions of pan-Sunnism against Iran, the champion of pan-Shi'ism, each with its own paranoia. Kuwait and eastern Saudi Arabia have sizeable Shi'i communities. Bahrain has a Shi'i majority. There are many Iranians in the UAE. In Oman, the majority of the population is Ibadi, an early offshoot of proto-Shi'ism. Zaydis are strong in Yemen. So all the way from southern Iraq, along the Gulf and round the peninsula to the lower end of the Red Sea, Saudi Arabia is ringed by a long belt of Shi'i sects. 'Alawis still hold power in Syria, and Hezbollah dominates much of Lebanon. South of Damascus, only Jordan lies between Saudi Arabia and another Shi'i arc to the north. Add to this anxiety the prospect of Iranian nuclear weapons, and you have all the ingredients of an escalating sectarian confrontation, since the Iranian regime thinks in the same way. The Iranians feel encircled by American pressure aiming to reduce them to submission to Western will. The result is a mutual paranoia which is fueling Sunni–Shi'i violence across the region.

The dynamic you describe substantially pre-dates the Arab Spring. How do you assess the Arab Spring's effect on these pre-existing antagonisms?

By cracking apart the old order without bringing forth any new one, it has simply created a more open field for militants. Currently, no Arab country has any real measure of stability. Egypt does not have it. Libya does not have it. Sudan does not have it. Jordan does not have it. Lebanon does not have it. Tunisia does not have it. Let alone Syria or Iraq. Nor is Saudi Arabia stable, after repressing Shi'i demonstrations for basic rights in its north-east, and sending troops into Bahrain in 2011 as soon as there was democratic unrest there. The one regional state that could have tried to mediate these conflicts was Turkey, but Erdoğan threw away his opportunities and now looks ridiculous with his own paranoid outbursts, blaming opposition protests at home on international conspiracies, on Kurds, and anyone who dares stand up to him.

How far has Israel, often portrayed as a modern Crusader state, played a role like that of the original Crusades in stoking religious passions across the region?

In a pan-Islamist perspective, Israel has always been a very small country with a very small population, which can be driven out as the Crusader states were, once the Muslim world is united. But every time the Arabs fought Israel, they lost. Ironically, in both Syria and Egypt, the war of 1973 is commemorated as a victory and celebrated as a national holiday, but of course they were both humiliated in that war. Yet the threat from Israel has never been a major factor in the popularization of Islamism. The vast majority of Arabs are hostile to Israel as a Jewish state. But this hostility is matched with a widespread indifference toward the Palestinians, whose cause has not been a central theme for Islamists. The fate of the Palestinians featured only in the margins of the thought of pan-Islamism's leading theorists. Even when it is invoked, Israel figures not as a major threat in itself, but as a proxy for the true threat: America and the West.

What really galvanized contemporary Islamism, and made it appealing, was the overthrow of the Shah in Iran. This was the first revolution in the region that succeeded in toppling a powerful ruler. No other change in the Muslim world has compared with that. The Algerian Revolution (1954–1962) was made against a colonial power: France. The ousting of the monarchy in Egypt (1952) was a tame coup d'état, like many of the same in Syria, Iraq, or Libya. In Iran, by contrast, massive popular demonstrations, sweeping aside the army, brought down the Shah: that was unprecedented. Who were the figures behind it? Khomeini and the mullahs. This boosted pan-Islamists' argument that religion can bring change. Islam is the alternative. An ideology, of which the trial runs by Mawdudi or Qutb had had a very limited reception, started to find a much wider and more willing audience.

In Afghanistan, Salafis jumped on the bandwagon, taking it in their own direction. In Egypt, Sadat used radical Sunni groups to weaken the popularity of socialists and communists in the universities and labor force. Then he realized they had become too powerful and he started cracking down

on them, especially after the Camp David peace with Israel
in 1978. This was a general pattern we see elsewhere. It was
pursued by the military regimes of the period, which sought
to appear in a good light as a barrier against two lunatic
elements (communists and Islamists), each manipulating
the other to destabilize it. Israeli intelligence did much the
same by fostering Hamas as a counterweight to Fatah in the
Palestinian territories. The US did the same in Afghanistan
by empowering jihadists against communists, but this backfired when these same jihadists started to target Americans.

*It seems a huge irony that visionaries who wanted a united
Islam should have helped set off the most violent division of
Islam of modern times. Accusations of apostasy — takfir — have
notoriously played a part in that. Where does this idea come
from?*

We find the term in Ibn Taymiyya in the thirteenth century
used against the recently converted Mongols and other
deviant Muslims, but its current usage is much more recent
and started with the Wahhabis. In principle, jihad cannot
be waged against fellow Muslims. So how could Salafis
mobilize people for a jihad against a ruler like Sadat or the
Saudi monarchs? The only way they could do it is to prove
that these rulers are no more Muslims. This is the essence
of Wahhabism. If we look at Osama Bin Laden's denunci-
ation of the stationing of American troops in Saudi Arabia
after the Gulf War, we see that his main point was to show

that the Saudi ruling family have become apostates. He was telling his followers: we need to fight jihad against them because they are no longer Muslims. By inviting enemies of Islam into the Holy Places they have abjured the faith. The same was true in Egypt. Salafis may be religious fanatics, but they have to observe basic Islamic law. You cannot cut corners, and simply urge your followers to wage jihad against fellow Muslims—you have to prove to them that these people are not Muslims anymore. So the mechanism of *takfir* is crucial to Salafism. You do not need any fatwa to kill infidels. But for Muslims, you not only need one, you need a fatwa explaining why they are no longer Muslims, and what they have done that has made them apostates.

That is why Lieutenant Islambouli, who shot Sadat in 1980, did not kill Mubarak at the same time. He could kill Sadat because Sadat was an apostate, but he did not have a fatwa to kill Mubarak. Conventional analysis of Islamic terrorism does not pay attention to what its militants actually say—it looks at economic factors or historical circumstances, operating with only a very general sense of religion and ideology, ignoring the precise terms in which they justify their actions. The head of the Law School at the University of Qatar addressing a Muslim audience once said the only way Islamic terrorism can be defeated is by understanding its theology and producing a counter to it. As long as we deny this, there is no way we can gain the upper hand over militant Islam.

The Zaydis are often held to be not only the oldest Shi'i com-
munity, but the dominant one in the Middle East until the
Buyids. If that is so, what explains their subsequent contrac-
tion to just the Yemeni edge of Arabia?

The Zaydis are the oldest sect within Shi'ism in the sense
that they were the first to shape its religious thought, already
in the late eighth and early ninth centuries. Until the tenth
century, they were popular in Iraq and north-western Iran.
Central to their theology was the belief that the imam, as
a religious and political leader, must prove his legitimacy
on the battlefield, by waging a victorious jihad. This meant
fighting other Muslims who had usurped power from the
rightful descendants of 'Ali. They also had looser criteria
whereby any descendant from 'Ali can be an imam (unlike
other Shi'i groups who restricted the imamate to descendants of 'Ali and Fatima from their son Husayn). Zaydis were
particularly prone to revolt. By contrast, after a few unsuc-
cessful and painful experiences, Twelver Shi'is opted for
a strategy of survival, lying low (what we term in Arabic
taqiyya) until the opportune conditions were lined up for a
rising. The Buyids who ruled Iraq and Iran for a century after
945 empowered all forms of Shi'ism, including the Zaydis;
however, they were politically savvy and took no systematic
measures against Sunnis. The Buyids were toppled in 1048
by the Seljuks, a Sunni confederation of Turkic nomads from
Central Asia, who adopted discriminatory policies against all
Shi'i groups with political aspirations. So many Zaydis had

little choice but to retreat to Yemen, which offered them a remote and mountainous refuge where they could hold out in a safe and supportive environment.

They had no previous connection with Yemen?

One of their key founders, Qasim al-Rassi (d. 860), lived in the area of Medina. In the late ninth century, his grandson Yahya (d. 911) was invited down to Yemen to arbitrate a tribal dispute, and established himself as an imam in the far north of the country. So yes, there was a Zaydi presence in Yemen. Later, in the eleventh century, to rejuvenate the theology of the local community, envoys were sent to Iraq and north-western Iran to encourage immigration of Zaydi scholars, at a time when Seljuk pressures were bearing down on all Shi'is. Zaydism would not have survived in Yemen without the influx of thinkers and books, including those written by the rationalist Mu'tazilas, which allowed Zaydism to sustain itself as an intellectually rigorous system. Subsequently, because of the isolation of their stronghold in the northern highlands of Yemen, some trends among the Zaydis became influenced by Sunnism. Sunnis would often say that among Shi'is, it is the Zaydis who are closest to them. That is because they have accommodated a lot of Shafi'i law and jurisprudence into their own practices, weakening the claim of the infallibility of the imam.

It was not until the Ottoman Empire disintegrated during the First World War that a Zaydi state covering the whole of Yemen, apart from the British colony of Aden in the far south, came into being, under an imam of a Zaydi clan called Mutawakkil. They ruled it as a kingdom until they were toppled in the 1960s by an officer coup, unleashing a civil war between royalist and republican forces that lasted for the better part of a decade.

In that conflict, the Saudi state was the principal backer of the Zaydi imamate in its fight to recover the power of the dynasty. Today, on the other hand, it is waging a ruthless bombing war on Zaydi forces in the Yemen. How far is a renewed sectarian zeal a motivating force in the Saudi campaign?

There is no doubt that the Shi'i–Sunni clash is at the heart of the current Saudi campaign in Yemen. In 2009, the mufti of Saudi Arabia declared that the Saudi soldiers who were fighting the Houthi rebels on the borders of Yemen were fighting jihad against infidels. So yes, we have there a sectarian war par excellence. But its significance, and its dynamics, have changed over time. Looking back, in Yemen itself there has long been a Zaydi–Sunni dichotomy. Most Sunnis are followers of the Shafi'i school, a tradition from which the Zaydis themselves took a lot. There has been as well tremendous variations of tribal allegiances, and divisions between regions and cities. During the civil war of the sixties, not a few Zaydis were republicans who had no sympathy for the royal family. For among Zaydis, anyone who claim a lineage from 'Ali is entitled to vie for leadership and there were many who were dissatisfied with the Mutawakkils. On top of that, in a period when traditional forms of rule in the Arab world were being brought down by young revolutionaries of one kind or another, Zaydis—like Muslims elsewhere, Shi'is or Sunnis—could be attracted to secular political ideologies, no longer defining their identity in religious terms but as nationalists, socialists, communists, Baathists, or whatever. This was a time when Shi'is in Iraq stopped seeing themselves as Shi'is and started seeing themselves as Iraqis, or Christians in the Arab world stopped seeing themselves as Christians and started seeing themselves as Arabs, no longer panicking at being a minority overwhelmed by Muslims. A secular identity trumped a sectarian identity.

In the Yemeni civil war of the sixties, the Saudis were scared by the growing popularity of the Egyptian president Jamal 'Abd-ul-Nasir (or Nasser) and his particular brand of Arab nationalism, which was popular throughout the Arab world. Nasser sent an army to North Yemen to support the republicans, so the Saudis stood behind the royalists. The Egyptian campaign was a complete failure and had to withdraw in 1967. By then a Marxist party had come to power in South Yemen, after the withdrawal of the British. This so alarmed the Saudis that they dropped their support of the royalists, who were operating from Saudi territory, and opted for a deal with the republicans in North Yemen (the North ultimately invaded the South and forced a unification in 1990). Alliances and animosities were not always strictly tied to Saudi religious zealotry, whose part in Saudi foreign policy waxed and waned according to broader strategic interests.

Conditions today differ altogether from the 1960s. Wahhabism then had no visible presence anywhere outside the Saudi kingdom, which had very little influence over Sunnis elsewhere. Now Wahhabi and Salafi militants are everywhere, and Saudi Arabia has become the reference point for many Sunnis as the one power that can stand up for them (a few exceptions withstanding), which puts many Sunnis at the mercy of Wahhabi manipulation. At the same time, Iran has been reaching out to all Shi'i groups across the Muslim world in the hope of drawing them into its own web of regional geopolitics. In Yemen, Iran started working vigorously on the Zaydis in the 1990s, funneling money to their organizations and inviting political activists to Iran to scheme against the Yemeni dictator 'Ali Saleh (r. 1978–2012). The Saudis struck back by helping Saleh to crush the Zaydis. This only rekindled the embers of civil war in Yemen. By 2012, Saleh had been in power for thirty-six years, and discontent with his rule boiled over in a Zaydi uprising in the north, which soon controlled most of the country, led by the influential Houthi family. When the uprising swept all over Yemen and Saleh was removed from power, he shifted alliances and lined up with Iran (blaming the Saudis for his ouster). At this point, the Saudis felt an Iranian dagger at their chest and intervened with an indiscriminate bombing campaign. On the other side of the conflict, 'Abd-ul-Malik al-Houthi, the leader of the Houthi rebels, is not simply following an

Iranian agenda. His entire political and religious legitimacy hinges on fighting and winning in Zaydi terms. If he wins, he will be the imam of Yemen. If he dies, he becomes a hero and a martyr. There is no third choice here.

Has Saudi Arabia really become the reference point for Sunnis everywhere in the Arab world? It certainly was not for Bin Laden. Is not there a trend within Salafism that is very hostile to the House of Saʿud, regarding it as hopelessly corrupt and in the pocket of Western imperialism? Would not that include the quite strong wing of al-Qaeda in Yemen?

Yes, to some extent this has become the case. It is true that now we have people who are Wahhabis in religious outlook, but do not have any political allegiance to the Saudis— indeed they are seeking to bring an end to the rule of the Saudi royal family. Some of these Wahhabis are definitely popular in Yemen. But if we look at most Salafis, most Sunni governments and the Sunni collective, there is a growing trend that they must line up with the Saudis because there is no other Sunni alternative. Also the Saudis still bet on the Wahhabi militants whom they cannot control anymore because they think they need them in the proxy war against Iran. This explains Saudi Arabia's support (secretive or otherwise) for groups such as ISIS.

After the series of events that we call the Arab Spring, Turkey under Erdoğan tried to become this new Sunni alternative and presented itself as the face of new Sunnism (and new Islam) in the world. Obama and the US loved this, and wanted to promote it as an alternative to militant Islam. For that, Erdoğan (and the US) found the Qataris willing to sponsor the project. This scenario came crashing as a result of the failed experiments in Egypt, Syria, Libya, and Tunisia where the Turkey–Qatari alliance has produced disastrous outcomes. The Saudis now have more control over the collective Sunni political impulse than ever before, and that is because we are witnessing an increasing Sunni paranoia toward Iran. It is as if the Shi'i century is coming back, and Sunnis, even those who in theory would not like the Saudis or Wahhabism, are lining up behind Saudi Arabia.

Could not one say that there is also, to some extent, an alternative pole to which embattled Sunnis can look for political aid and support, in Qatar? Has not the Al Thani dynasty there been a major patron and backer of the Muslim Brotherhood in Egypt, and in general taken its own line in current conflicts in the Arab world?

Yes, the Qataris have always tried to distinguish themselves from the Saudis—they hate to have the role of second fiddle to Riyadh and their political philosophy until very recently reflected that. The Qataris gave this a very active push, with plenty of money, a widely watched television station (Al Jazeera), and some air-power to back it up. But the suppression of the Muslim Brothers in Egypt by General Sisi was a big setback for Qatar, which had backed them, and the current

Emir is walking a tightrope trying not to offend Saudi Arabia, which he realizes could be imprudent in the long run. The other Gulf states, grouped in the UAE, are dependencies of Saudi power—some, like Abu Dhabi, are also Wahhabi— and are all calculating that if they look ten or twenty years down the road, they might need Saudi troops to keep them in power. The dynasty in Bahrain, where the majority of the population is Shi'i, has already required Saudi intervention to survive. The UAE serves as a loyal auxiliary for the Saudis in Yemen, supplying funds, planes and troops for the effort to bring down the Houthi government in San'a, while the Gulf Cooperation Council—which includes Qatar— provides diplomatic cover for the operation.

How does the Kuwaiti monarch stand vis-à-vis Wahhabism?

There is a significant Shi'i minority in Kuwait, and there are some Salafis there too. But the Sunnism of most Kuwaitis is Maliki and not Wahhabi, and the Al Sabah dynasty tries to adopt a position like its Hashemite counterpart in Jordan, avoiding too close alignment with the Saudi monarchy. Yet the Kuwaitis know where regional power lies. That is why Kuwait had to break relations with Iran this year (2016), after the execution of a Shi'i cleric in the Qatif region (northeast Saudi Arabia) led to an attack on the Saudi embassy in Tehran. The Al Sabah ruling family has not forgotten the key role the Saudis played in organizing its restoration to power in 1991 after Saddam drove them out of the country.

Would the aloof position of the Omani Sultanate, keeping its distance from the Saudi kingdom and preserving discreet relations with Iran, be related to its Ibadi denomination? In religious terms, can Ibadi doctrine be regarded as equidistant from Sunnism and Shi'ism?

Ibadism traces its roots all the way back to the very first sect that was formed in the late 650s, called Khawarij, a movement formed by supporters of 'Ali who rebelled against him for accepting negotiations with Mu'awiya, and killed him in 661, which opened the way for Mu'awiya to become caliph. At the beginning, the Khawarij were very militant and declared all Muslims who did not join them apostates. This caused their widespread popular and intellectual alienation, and they were largely treated as outcasts. Over time, and under the pressure of wars waged against them by more mainstream Muslims, the sect retreated from its original bases in southern Iraq and western Iran to Morocco—where it flourished for some years in the ninth century—and more durably to Oman, where it reinvented itself as a moderate movement called Ibadism and has survived to this day. Because they consider themselves to predate the formation of Shi'ism and Sunnism, the Ibadis invariably position themselves above the Sunni–Shi'i schism, and maintain good relations with everybody.

What of the Iranian view of Saudi Arabia, then? Could the relations between the two be described as asymmetrical, in the sense that, historically, there was never any counterpart to the savagery of the Wahhabi destruction of Shi'i shrines in lower Iraq and accompanying massacres? Is the memory of this still alive in Iran today, or just a dim reference in schoolbooks, essentially irrelevant to contemporary rivalry between the two countries?

I think it is very, very relevant. Naturally, there will be political figures in Iran who invoke this history without inwardly attaching much importance to it, as one would expect of politicians in any inter-state rivalry. But there are lots of people in Iran for whom this is a living history that continues to this day. When 400 Iranian pilgrims to Mecca were killed by the Saudi riot police in 1987, their deaths immediately brought back what the Wahhabis did to the Shi'is and their shrines in 1801 and 1802, and the Sunnis did to Imam Hussein in 680 (a similar incident occurred in Mecca in 2015). Suddenly all these episodes were relived together, and under their spell popular reaction was clear. Does every mullah in Iran hold fast to their connection? I do not think so. But enough mullahs do to inform Iranian foreign policy. Official propaganda exploits this history, which resonates deep down in a wide popular audience and is entrenched in the Shi'i religious psychology.

What explains the puzzle of the latter-day absence of Shi'i communities in the Maghreb, when in the tenth and eleventh centuries the Fatimid Caliphate covered virtually the whole of North Africa?

What is roughly now Morocco and western Algeria were ruled between the 780s and 920s by a Zaydi dynasty called the Idrisids. They were Arabs, but their power depended on pacts with local Berber tribes. In the ninth century, their rule was challenged by a Khawarij group, ancestors of the Ibadis. In the early tenth century, this Khawarij group was essentially eliminated by the Fatimids, an Isma'ili branch of Shi'ism which forged a successful alliance with Berber tribes in what is today Tunisia, which gave them enough manpower to spread across North Africa and conquer Egypt, extending their rule into Syria and western Arabia (the Hijaz). Under the Fatimid Caliphate in Cairo, which lasted until 1171 when it was overthrown by Saladin, Isma'ili Shi'ism was popular throughout their realms, including Syria. But settling down in a much richer region of the Arab world, the Fatimids became less interested in North Africa and dissociated from their original base among the Berbers.

Why did Shi'ism then disappear in North Africa after the Fatimids? A similar pattern has puzzled scholars of Late Antiquity—the complete disappearance of Christianity from North Africa in the seventh century after the expulsion of the Byzantine Empire. The answer seems to lie in a dynamic typical of nomadic societies: the propensity of entire tribes to move swiftly and collectively from one religion or sect to another. The simple explanation for the disappearance of Shi'ism in North Africa is that Berber society tended to convert wholesale, transferring from one belief system to the next. Subsequent rulers of the Maghreb were Sunnis, and Berbers adapted to them; and since no Shi'i dynasty invaded North Africa thereafter, they remained Sunnis. In Egypt itself, the disappearance of Shi'ism was less spontaneous. There Saladin and his Ayyubid successors (1171–1250), pursued an aggressive campaign of Sunnification, confiscating Shi'i institutions and turning them into Sunni seminaries or mosques. This policy was continued by the Mamluk dynasty (1250–1517). The Azhar, for example, was founded as a Shi'i seminary to train Isma'ili preachers and missionaries, and send them out to convert other Muslims. It was state repression that stamped out Shi'ism in Egypt, where today there are no Isma'ilis and the handful of Shi'is are recent immigrants.

Would it be wrong to think that Sufism occupies a role not altogether unlike Shi'ism in the Maghreb—and Muslim Black Africa—as a strain of heterodoxy at odds with rigorist forms of Sunnism?

The term heterodoxy should be avoided. I myself come from a Sunni background, but I object to scholars, or ordinary people, terming non-Sunni groups heterodox, since it gives the impression that Sunnis are good Muslims and the other Muslims are less legitimate. This is historically quite wrong. From the minute the Prophet Muhammad died, Muslims disagreed as to how Islam should be defined. Even Muhammad did not establish a clear definition of Islam. He told different people different things, and by the admission of countless

Muslim medieval scholars, his teachings are not coherent, which partly explains the fragmentation within Islam.

It is true that Sufism and Shi'ism are at odds with rigorist forms of Sunnism. But, for the record, one has to say that moderate Sunnis are also at odds with rigorist forms of Sunnism. Sufism is a movement originating in the ninth century that became popular among Sunnis because traditional Sunnism is very dry and legalistic and focused on living according to God's law. That is why we call each of the five main divisions within Sunni Islam *madhhab*, which literally translates as "the way." Each prescribes the right way to live and to practice Islam, and so is mostly concerned with laws and rules. Hence, each has its own Shari'a. These schools are not interested in issues of spiritual life because these issues are not questions that jurisprudence can regulate, enumerate, or quantify. Sufism, on the other hand, is about the life of the spirit. At the beginning, it was at odds with mainstream Sunnism because Sunni jurists saw it as a way to bypass Shari'a. When they realized that Sunnism could not survive without a spiritual dimension, they accepted Sufism as one of the philosophical/theological components of Sunnism.

Why has Sufism historically been principally, although not exclusively, a Sunni phenomenon? Would it be because Shi'ism is in some ways a more emotional creed than Sunnism, one in which suffering and mourning are iconically more central, so less in need of a distinctive spiritual complement?

Sufism is based on the belief that any human being can through mystical reflection be in direct communion with God. Traditional Sunnism focuses on orthopraxy: salvation is attained by strict adherence to the law, to prayer, to fasting, etc. Since spiritualism does not have anything to do with law, traditional Sunnism does not say much about it. Sunnis are supposed to do good works to guarantee their admission to Paradise at the end of times. Sufis do not want to wait that long. They want to get to Paradise now. Thus, an emotional void in traditional Sunnism is filled by Sufism, which in this respect is not an orthopraxy but rather an orthodoxy. As such, Sufism is primarily concerned with proper beliefs. Shi'ism is also primarily an orthodoxy—one must believe that the imam is divinely chosen and receives divine communication; here we can broadly compare traditional Sunnism to Judaism (the primacy of law), and traditional Sufism and Shi'ism to Christianity (primacy of faith). It should be said that when Sufism became popular, Shi'is started to appropriate it as well. The Safavids and the Alevis are tremendously influenced by Sufism.

The popularity of Sufism became manifest when average Sunnis realized they needed more than prayer and fasting, and the like. They needed direct avenues to God to involve him in their lives and to seek his intervention. Sufi masters who attain union with God become living saints. In Sufi language, they are God's hands to spread his graces and miracles into this world. So it is very popular among Muslims who are attracted to Sufism to visit Sufi saints—and if these saints are dead, to visit their tombs—in order to receive divine grace. This is an outrage to Salafis, who attack Sufi shrines because they consider them a form of paganism that corrupts Islam.

Among the major schools of Sunnism, the Maghreb is over-whelmingly Maliki in affiliation. What distinguishes the five principal madhhabs, and what explains the geographical distribution of their respective following?

Sunnism started as a trend among scholars in early Islam who emphasized that to be a Muslim is to model oneself on the acts of the Prophet Muhammad and his companions. Many sought to define this as an orthopraxy or set of rules and rituals, which gave rise to the schools of Shari'a or madhhabs. Often it was the disciples of a teacher who developed his views and launched a school. In the span of a century, there were so many of them, spread all over the Muslim world, that the Abbasid caliph Mutawakkil (r. 847–861) decided that a limit must be placed on the number of such schools. As noted earlier, five Sunni schools were sanctioned. They were the Hanafi school after Abu Hanifa (d. 767), the Maliki school after Malik ibn Anas (d. 795), the Shafi'i school after Shafi'i (d. 820), the Hanbali school after Ahmad ibn Hanbal (d. 855), and the Zahiri school after Dawud al-Zahiri (d. 884). There was also one Shi'i school sanctioned: the Ja'fari school named after Imam Ja'far al-Sadiq (d. 765). Over time, the Zaydi school was accepted as well.

Sunnis were hence expected to "belong" to one of the sanctioned Sunni schools (a new one emerged in India in the nineteenth century called the Ahmadiyya). Each had its network of jurists and lawyers. The Hanafi school emphasized the need to devise laws in light of the jurist's duty to decide what was generally good for Muslims in a given situation/context. It appealed primarily to non-Arabs, and today is found mainly in Central Asia, India, and Turkey, as well as parts of the Arab Middle East. The Maliki school stipulated that Muslims must imitate the example of the first Muslim community in Medina, and flourished primarily in the western Islamic world, from Libya to Morocco and through to medieval Spain. The Shafi'i school emphasized the need to adhere to the Sunna of Prophet Muhammad and devise laws in relation to a system of jurisprudence. It flourished in the Arab world, in Yemen, India, and Indonesia. The Hanbali school was a puritanical reaction to what its founder considered as anti-Islamic practices. It insisted that God's laws should not be altered or manipulated in order to please people and conform to their needs. Until modern times and the rise of Salafism, it was the least popular in Islam. Wahhabism came out of the Hanbali school, and the spread of Wahhabism and Salafism allowed the Hanbali school to reach places where it never had a foothold before. The Zahiri school was the most literalist, disliking the speculations and legal theories that jurists often pursue. Though it was once popular in North Africa and Spain, now only negligible groups in Morocco and Pakistan still adhere to it.

These Sunni schools did not develop a theology, with the single exception of the Hanbalis. They focused just on Shariʻa (laws, rituals, and practices). If their followers were interested in theology, they had to shop somewhere else. This allowed competing theological trends to flourish. For example, in the medieval period the followers of the Shafiʻi school split into sharply divided theological camps—Ashʻarism, after the theologian Ashʻari (d. 936), Maturidism, after the theologian Maturidi (d. 944), Muʻtazilism (a movement that flourished from the eighth to the twelfth century), Sufism, etc. It was in this theological leeway that Sufism became very popular among Sunnis. The Hanbalis alone developed their own creed, which was literalist and puritanical. One of their most contentious tenets was physical anthropomorphism: God has a hand and a face because the Qurʼan says so (e.g., 5.64), an idea rejected by other Muslims who held these passages to be metaphorical.

The differential spread of these schools of law was connected to factors like population movements, missionary activities, trading patterns. For instance, Shafiʻism became popular in Indonesia and coastal South Asia because it was introduced by Shafiʻi merchants from Egypt and Yemen. Hanafism took root among Turkic peoples of Central Asia, arriving in Anatolia with the Seljuks and the Ottomans who sponsored the spread of Hanafism throughout their empire. Hence, most Turks in contemporary Turkey are theoretically Hanafis. Each school required state sponsorship and a legal apparatus for it to flourish and compete with its rivals.

Otherwise, people deserted it for another school. With the downfall of the Almohads in Spain and North Africa, the Zahiris were left with no sponsor and their followers dwindled away. Nevertheless, in most major cities in the Middle East in pre-modern times (e.g., Aleppo, Damascus, Cairo, Alexandria, Baghdad, etc.), all of these schools had a presence. Today, however, it is important to understand that many Muslims have no idea as to what school of law they belong. This is one of the consequences of modernization, and the collapse of traditional religion in most Muslim societies.

Are there particular characteristics of Maliki Islam that remain relevant to its dominance in the Maghreb and sub-Saharan Africa?

In pre-modern societies, war was as much part of daily life as peace, and religion adapted itself to reflect both. Today we want to believe that religion is about peace and love, but this reflects modern agendas rather than the historical reality of almost all religions. There were many militant Maliki movements throughout Islamic history. For example, in the eleventh century a powerful jihadi force rose up in the Maghreb and swept through North Africa and Spain. They are called Almoravids (who took their name from the word *marabout*, which refers to Sufi dwellings). They were Maliki Berbers influenced by Sufism, and their rule lasted until 1147, when they were upstaged by a more militant group called Almohads, who remained in power until 1269. In modern times, another such movement erupted in Libya in reaction to Italian occupation, led by Umar al-Mukhtar (d. 1931), a slave-trader by profession.

That said, what facilitated the spread of Maliki Sunnism in the Maghreb and sub-Saharan Africa was its version of Shari'a that included two important juridical principles which made it particularly adaptable to different environments. These were 'urf (local customs) and istislah (public good), and their consequence was that Maliki jurists did not apply exactly the same laws in every setting. They took into consideration the local customs and what was generally in the best interests of the community. This made Maliki rulings well suited to Berber and sub-Saharan culture. For example, Maliki Shari'a stipulates that a woman can become pregnant up to five years after she has had sex with her husband. How can this be possible? The Maliki explanation is that an embryo may lie dormant for five years. No other school of law in Islam has a conception remotely like this. Maliki jurists came up with this idea (which could be based on an old custom in North Africa) in order to address a problem in Berber societies where men were accustomed to leaving their families for long periods of warfare or caravan trade. It was an ingenious way of explaining "strange" pregnancies, to protect women from being stoned for adultery. To maintain the public good, they adopted the theory of the dormant embryo.

The Salafism that made its appearance in Algeria in the 1990s was an intrusion into a Maliki setting?

Yes, the violence in Algeria when the army and the Front Islamique du Salut (FIS) plunged the country into a civil war was a product of the misbegotten policies of the military regime in Algeria, which in the 1970s invited thousands of Egyptian preachers to take over local mosques in the country in order to weaken indigenous Maliki Islamists. Some of these preachers were Salafis, who injected an outlook hitherto foreign to Algerian culture and religious life. In 1989, Algerian Salafis formed the FIS as a political party and a year later they won the elections. The Algerian regime reacted by staging a bloody coup, and the Salafis obliged, committing some of the worst atrocities in any Muslim country up to that time.

Is the importance of the Marabouts in Saharan and sub-Saharan Africa specific to the region, or do they represent simply a regional variation of cults of local saints or holy men common to Sufism across the Muslim world?

The Marabouts are both a variant of a widespread phenomenon in the Muslim world and a phenomenon specific to North Africa and sub-Saharan Africa. They became popular there because they did not radically depart from the roles traditionally played by local shamans and sorcerers in the pre-Islamic religions of North and West Africa. Sufism has a fascinating ability to blend in with local customs. We see this on spectacular display in South Asian cultures where Sufism is very similar to Hinduism and Buddhism in its use of music, songs, images, etc. The Marabouts took their inception from Sufism. But they lack the scholarly tradition for which Sufism in Egypt, Syria, Iraq, Iran, Central Asia, or India is famous. The reason is that in these regions Sufism was competing with other well-formed currents and had to develop a serious intellectual side to appeal to scholars. In Berber and sub-Saharan African societies, there was not so much of an intellectual tradition, so in comparison all forms of Islam in Saharan and sub-Saharan Africa, including the Marabouts, are less intellectually rigorous than groups in other parts of the Muslim world.

What might explain the exceptional strength and importance of Sufi brotherhoods as a form of religious community in sub-Saharan Africa? Is there any equivalent of a phenomenon like the Mourides of Senegal elsewhere in the world of Islam?

African society (on both sides of the Sahara) was a perfect environment for Sufism. People there could not live according to the dictates of traditional Sunnism. Sometimes we forget that traditional Sunnism is the creation of a class of urban elites. The way they envisaged Islam reflected their priorities, worldviews, and conditions. This did not always work in rural societies. Sufism represents the exact opposite: God can choose someone to be his envoy in the world who comes from a wretched background, who cannot even read or write. For the modest and the poor, that was huge: God cares about us too, even though we are imperfect and can barely do what official religion tells us to do. Also, Sufism formed and spread around brotherhoods (called *tariqa* or "the way"). Each brotherhood followed a saint guiding its members toward God. With the emergence of modernity, Sufism was battered down in some societies as it came to be seen as old-fashioned and anti-reform. But in other societies, it succeeded in transforming itself. The Mourides were one of those successful cases. In the nineteenth century, they emerged in Senegal and surrounding lands as at once a religious movement calling for reforms of the faith, and a political movement opposing French colonialism. They were not unique. You see similar phenomena elsewhere in the Muslim world. For example, in Libya another Sufi movement, the Sanusiyya, also emerged as a force for both religious reform and resistance to foreign rule.

But were the two so similar? Could not one speak rather of a spectrum of ferment in the nineteenth century, with the Mourides — a Sufi brotherhood that never took up arms against the French, prospered under their rule, and eventually became something like a wealthy multinational business corporation — at one end, and the messianic movement of the Mahdi against the Egyptians and the British in Sudan — crushed by Kitchener with a large army — at the other end, with the Sanusiyya — who rejected the apocalyptic authority of the Mahdi, but were a lot more combative than the Mourides — in the middle?

Yes, there were such differences. The Mourides focused on building a network of commerce, and in this way they were different from most other groups. Other reform movements focused too much on politics. The common pattern throughout was the emergence of movements of reform on the periphery of Islam blending various mixtures of traditionalist religion, messianism, and mysticism, and frequently engaging in jihad. In sub-Saharan Africa, we also had the Fulani Caliphate of Sokoto (1809–1903) founded by Usman dan Fodio spreading across what is now northern Nigeria; their legacy is one of the factors still fueling animosity between Muslims and Christians there today. The Sanusiyya movement, which fought the French, British, and Italian colonial presence, extended all the way to Chad and Niger. In Central Asia, there was the Naqshbandi revolt against Chinese domination in Xinjiang that lasted until 1877; its memory is still present in Uyghur resistance to the PRC. Each of these movements had its own geographical context, but can be seen as part of a broad trend sweeping round the outer edges of the Muslim world, where central authority was weak, the political and religious scene was fragmented, and there was a felt need to fend off non-Muslim encroachment on Muslim lands. Where these movements took a violent millennial turn, as in the Sudan with a lot of brutality against Christians and animist Africans, they failed for familiar reasons: the unpopularity of excessive militancy and repressive austerity, and a realization that the eschaton is not coming.

In the core regions of the Muslim world, you have said that in the eighteenth and nineteenth centuries, impulses of reform in Islam could take either a modernizing or an archaizing direction—one more liberal, the other proto-Salafi—and that in this period both typically remained confined to small intellectual circles, with the exception of Wahhabism, which alone generated a mass movement. What about the other wing of reformist Islam in the twentieth century? Would you classify the Muslim Brotherhood as a successful translation of this impulse into a mass movement?

The beginning of the twentieth century was not kind to Muslim reform movements in general. Not a few emerged, but the overall environment was pushing Muslims away from religion. Many Muslims considered Islam to be the reason for their inferiority to the West, and were eager to get on the bandwagon of Westernization and modernization, opting for other ideologies. Opposite to them were the Salafis who blamed the Muslims for having weakened Islam. Liberal Islamists tried to split the blame between Islam and the Muslims, which at first was not very effective, helping to explain why their ideas failed to translate into mass movements. The Brotherhood was arguably the first real breakthrough to a successful modernism. Its founder Hassan al-Banna was not a religious scholar—he was a schoolteacher. Likewise, the overwhelming majority of the leaders of the Brotherhood since his time have not been trained clerics. Moreover, Banna never declared other Muslims to be infidels, a defining characteristic of modern Salafism. He did not denounce Shiʿis, telling his followers to steer clear of divisive issues that set Muslims against each other. There is no takfir in his writings.

The movement he created in the 1920s appealed to the poor, but more importantly to an emerging Egyptian middle class, which under the monarchy—that is, up to the turn of the 1950s—enjoyed a relative freedom of expression and of the press unique in the Middle East at the time. For several decades from the 1870s to the 1940s, Egypt was the intellectual hub of the Arab world, attracting writers and thinkers from all over the region—who founded many leading newspapers and periodicals. It was in this liberal climate, in which ideas were debated, not just proclaimed, that the Brotherhood was formed. The political system itself was narrower and more repressive than this cultural space, so though the Brotherhood was in effect a movement of political aspiration, the infrastructure it built focused on the creation of a network of educational and welfare services in civil society, rather than on direct bids to gain state power. Its adherents were also encouraged to go into business, where many did very well. In a sense, it was its degree of displacement from the political arena that liberated it to construct a mass movement with these distinctively modern characteristics.

There is something else that is important about the religious philosophy of the Brotherhood. The movement emphasized the need for its followers to be better Muslims, with the focus on Islamic dress, attending prayers, attending

Brotherhood-sanctioned schools, doing business as much as possible with other members, etc. For them, that was a fundamental step in fighting the corruption of Western lifestyle and education.

But, ideologically speaking, was not the line between modernism and fundamentalism quite blurred in the Brotherhood's version of Islam?

From fairly early on, there were two theological and political tendencies within the Brotherhood, one that was moderate and the other that was militant. Historically, the former was always dominant, even in post-war years when there were unauthorized outbreaks of militancy which brought the authorities down on them—in 1948 Banna paid with his life for one of these. But when Nasser consolidated his power in the 1950s, the organization—which he came to regard as a major threat to his regime—for the first time suffered mass repression, with the imprisonment of thousands of its members, and the torture of many. In jail, one of these, Sayyid Qutb—also a schoolteacher and a contemporary of Banna—was a well-known writer and thinker. Qutb developed a full-blown Salafi doctrine, complete with the need for hijra, the mechanism of takfir, and consignment of all Muslims as living in an age of Jahiliyya—the pagan darkness in which Arabs lived before the coming of Muhammad, into which not even Ibn Taymiyya had cast them. Invoking Jahiliyya meant that the very few remaining good Muslims must learn from the experience of Muhammad that the only way to deal with Jahiliyya is by fighting it and utterly destroying it. *Milestones*, the book in which Qutb set out these ideas, was a more electrifying literary work than any publication by Banna, and became a touchstone for younger militants after Qutb's execution by Nasser in 1966. Many of these militants fled to Saudi Arabia, among them Qutb's younger brother Muhammad, who became a teacher of Bin Laden (Sayyid Qutb himself had been a tutor in the family of Ayman Zawahiri, who replaced Bin Laden as leader of al-Qaeda). Later, the fervent youngsters exported by Mubarak to Afghanistan in the 1980s would be reinforcements for this faction when they came home. The result was a split in the organization. A militant wing folded into or aligned themselves with Wahhabism and militant Salafism. Their exit allowed the moderate factions of the Brotherhood to take complete charge and lower the organization's political visibility.

But if one looks at the ultimate objectives of the two wings, were they so different? The detailed ethnography in Hazim Kandil's recent work on the Brotherhood speaks of its driving religious determinism—the belief that if it simply created a community of the godly here and now, divine intervention would assure it of not only economic success, already achieved, but political victory, without it having to strive directly for this.[1] If that were

---

1   Hazem Kandil, *Inside the Brotherhood* (Malden, 2015), pp. 82–7 et seq.

so, would not the dividing line between the Brotherhood and Salafis have less to do with the difference between modernizing and archaizing conceptions of religious rejuvenation, than with the contrast between a passive attentiste and an active voluntarist version of fundamentalism?

To some extent, yes, there is a sense of determinism, and this is classical in most religions: if God is on your side you will eventually win. Nevertheless, the Brotherhood had to compete with extremist ideas on the street, and in doing so started to echo some of them in much the way that, say, Republican candidates for the US presidency from immigrant backgrounds will pick up xenophobic themes today because that is what galvanizes the Republican voters. It never went much deeper than this—genuine militancy always remained a weak trend within the organization. When popular rebellion erupted against Mubarak in 2011, the Brotherhood initially played no part in it. When it became clear that Mubarak would be ousted, they were tempted. They saw in the elections after his fall a unique opportunity to control the political scene, which history might never give them again. But with no prior experience and a lot of arrogance, the Brotherhood soon alienated the rest of Egyptian society, making it easy for the army to topple them. Here I think they were betting on Obama and the US to keep them in power.

The military, however, needed ideological cover for its seizure of power, and there the ecumenical position of the

Brotherhood in religious matters, standing above Sunni–Shi'i antagonisms, backfired against it. The Saudis were a close ally of Mubarak when he repressed the Brotherhood, and were far from pleased when he was overthrown and the Brotherhood came to power. The hostility was reciprocal: in office, the Brotherhood made a point of reaching out to Iran rather than to Saudi Arabia. When General Sisi mounted his coup against Morsi and unleashed a bloody crackdown on the Brotherhood, the Egyptian Salafis—who had emerged as an electoral force in competition with them—got orders from the Saudis to go along with it. In the Saudi view, the Egyptian army is a bulwark against the Brotherhood, for the moment. They are completely behind Sisi, telling the local Salafis (represented in the Nour Party) they must bide their time. This explains why the Salafis and the Brotherhood in Egypt now stand in completely opposite camps. The Salafis are aligned with the brutal dictatorship of Sisi and the Brotherhood has been driven underground—literally and figuratively. Needless to say, there are other militant Salafis who are fighting the Egyptian army in Sinai. These are a different bunch that answers no more to the Saudis.

The Brotherhood was a presence not just in Egypt but across much of the Arab world. How strong have been the bonds with its affiliates elsewhere? Has it historically had any organizational control over them?

The Brotherhood outgrew Egypt, but it did so not by deliberate creation from Cairo, but by local imitation. The only exception was the Egyptian diaspora, significant in the UAE, Qatar, Kuwait, Saudi Arabia, and Libya, even in Nigeria. There the Brotherhood was active in expatriate communities composed of teachers and technicians, who were often quite prosperous and could supply funds as well as recruits to the center in Egypt. Elsewhere, they were autonomous, each organization reflecting local conditions in the country where it operated. What they had in common was the strategy for success they learnt from Egypt: the building of a network of welfare institutions, designed especially to appeal to merchants and college graduates, as the social carapace disguising a political movement. In some places like Lebanon, they did not even call themselves Ikhwan, they were known as 'Ubbad al-Rahman (Worshipers of the Merciful). When my father first came to Beirut at the age of fourteen, he joined for a year a boy-scout organization which was operated by them—he had no idea it was a Brotherhood outfit till much later. Politically speaking, in a country like Jordan, the Brotherhood hewed closely to the moderate path taken in Egypt, on the whole placating the monarchy and reining in younger radicals when they threatened to rebel against it; at various times, they even had not a few ministers in the king's cabinet. But pacifism was by no means always the case. The Brotherhood in Syria displayed no trace of religious determinism. It staged a fierce armed rising against Hafez Assad in Hama, which he flattened with a wholesale massacre, leveling a good part of the city with tanks and artillery. The Syrian Brotherhood also took the lead in the early fighting against Bashar Assad in the current civil war, before being overtaken by Salafi forces. Likewise in Palestine: Hamas, which came out of the Palestinian Brotherhood movement, is hardly either a passive or a pacifist group. The different directions taken by the Brotherhood organizations are typically dependent on the local context.

Would the Gülen movement in Turkey be another example of the organizational crystallization of a modernizing outlook?

Yes, that is another case, but it is a rather recent case. There were several Turkish movements preceding Gülen's organization. They focused primarily on political change, such as Necmettin Erbakan's successive parties in the 1970s and 1990s. But these were all met with political repression by the secular state in Turkey, which tried to push many Islamists away from politics, leading them to adopt the alternative strategy of building a strong social and financial network, like that of the Brotherhood, that could at a later point be used to stage a political comeback. That was the genesis of the Gülen movement. President Erdoğan, who came to power with its help, understands this very well and has since turned violently against the movement, whose supporters were infiltrating all strata of the Turkish state and society, and—in his view—plotting against him, especially now after the failed coup attempt.

Have modernist trends in Islam shown any pattern like the various attempts at a triage of scriptures, elevating some and downgrading others, which you find in Reformation Christianity? Would the ideas, for example, of Mahmoud Taha in Sudan, or his pupil Abdullahi an-Na'im, be of this kind? If so, are they pretty marginal, or not untypical?

Modernist trends in Islam are all over the shop in terms of intellectual coherence and objectives. It is not easy to argue that a seventh-century ideology is fit for twentieth- or twenty-first-century societies. Yet one main theme has been quite consistent throughout. Almost all reform movements have fallen into what we might call the Protestant trap—namely, the belief that Islam can be modernized by returning to the Qur'an. But the Qur'an on its own will get the Muslims nowhere. Medieval Muslims realized this very early on and pushed the Qur'an into a ceremonial role. The Protestant Reformation was against the Church of Rome and its politics of religion. There is no such thing as a Roman Church in Sunni Islam. Sunni thinkers who insisted that the Qur'an could empower modernization soon became bogged down in a conceptual quagmire that explains the crisis in Islamic thought today. The Qur'an legitimizes a lot of things that modern Muslims consider embarrassing: slavery, military jihad, control of women, polygamy, scientific fallacies (e.g., the sun sets in a pool of lava: 18.86), etc. Consequently, many modern thinkers who cling to a Protestant approach to scripture argue that the way forward is to recover the "spirit" of the Qur'an. This move allows a scholar to decide that the spirit of the Qur'an promotes social justice, and the entire text can therefore be reinterpreted accordingly or ignored. In so doing, modern reformers have realized the limitation of the Qur'an but only after they butchered the best thing about Islam: the fascinating civilization that Muslims have created over the centuries, with its curiosity about knowledge and science, its religious pluralism, the flexibility of Shari'a, and the great diversity that went with that.

Mahmoud Taha (d. 1985) was a Sudanese thinker who tried to propose a solution for Islam and modernism. He argued that the Qur'an contains two messages: one revealed to the Prophet Muhammad in Mecca, and another revealed to him in Medina. The reason for the two is that God realized that the Muslims were incapable of grasping the message of Mecca, so he sent them a watered-down version, which comprises the message of Medina. This was a compromise designed to help Muhammad win over supporters, which allowed certain practices and customs to persist even though they were, properly speaking, un-Islamic. The message of Medina was meant to be only temporary, until a generation of Muslims emerged who could understand the original message of Mecca and practice Islam in its true form (according to Taha, the only person who had ever done so was Muhammad himself). Taha believed that the twentieth century was going to see the birth of this new Muslim generation. Since he was essentially telling his contemporaries that they were not practicing Islam correctly, his views did not endear him to many. He was hanged for apostasy by the Nimeiry dictatorship (1971–1985) in 1985.

Abdullahi an-Naʿim, now a professor at Emory University, is a notable thinker of Islamic humanism, much influenced by Taha. He refined the message of Taha by arguing that Muslims must move past classical Shariʿa in order to introduce a system that de-Islamizes such horrible institutions as slavery, legal subjugation of religious minorities, limitation of human rights, etc. Essentially An-Naʿim is saying that Shariʿa worked in medieval times and was intended for medieval times, but is now completely unsuitable for the modern age. The stunning thing is that virtually every Muslim government of the twentieth century, with the exception of one or two, have agreed with him, but very few have ever dared say so in public. If we look at Muslim countries today, they all have Western-style constitutions and restrict the application of Shariʿa law to matters of personal law (marriage, divorce, inheritance, etc.). If Muslims believe Shariʿa is still relevant, why do they have constitutions and legal institutions that operate under a different legal system and philosophy?

The appeal of the views of thinkers like Taha and an-Naʿim is limited because most Islamic thought today is generated in a politically charged environment where a Muslim thinker can be accused of treason if he or she argues against what is perceived as Islamic solidarity. There is a widespread trend of apologetics, present even in Western academia, that tries to exonerate Islam from all "embarrassing" views and teachings, and marginalizes and vilifies Muslim reformers who say otherwise. Figures like Taha and an-Naʿim have been persecuted or marginalized because they say that Muslims and their faith are partly responsible for many practices that are incompatible with the ideals of modernity.

What is the standing of the hadith predicting an apocalyptic victory of the faithful over the Byzantines that looms large in the outlook of ISIS? How widely would it have been known, and how often was it invoked in earlier periods?

There is a strange apocalyptic hadith attributed to the Prophet Muhammad which predicts that the Day of Judgment will not come until a Byzantine army marches to the field of Dabiq, a small town to the north of Aleppo in Syria, where an army from Medina, featuring the best Muslims on earth, will fight them. When the two armies square off, one group of Muslims will run away; these God will never pardon. Another group will die as martyrs; these are the best martyrs in God's eyes. A third group will be victorious and proceed to conquer Constantinople. While the Muslims are collecting booty there, the Antichrist will appear. They will rush back to fight him, and that is when Jesus will return to earth and join the Muslims to kill the Antichrist. At that point, the Day of Judgment commences. This hadith is very well known in apocalyptic literature and is cited in many hadith collections. Any Muslim who is familiar with the Hadith and Islamic apocalypticism knows this hadith very well.

To what extent has it informed the military strategy of ISIS?

Today, the idea of the Day of Judgment has all but disappeared from public conversation about religion, especially among scholars and the intelligentsia. In classical religion and for people who practice religion in the classical sense, the Day of Judgment is a reality that guides their world and informs their religious anxieties. When ISIS invokes this hadith and the memory of Dabiq, it is essentially reminding Muslims of three incredibly powerful religious imageries: 1) This is *the* apocalyptic battle that Muhammad prophesied; 2) Muslims who do not join the battle will never be pardoned by God; 3) in joining, Muslims have their last opportunity for salvation, because when the Day of Judgment arrives, they will have no more chances.

ISIS employs this memory very powerfully and effectively. The movement even calls its monthly magazine *Dabiq*. The tremendous symbolism of Dabiq and this hadith explain the reasons why ISIS has pushed to occupy Raqqa and make it their temporary capital. Their objective is not Raqqa itself. They need Raqqa as a base to prepare an assault on Aleppo, because squaring off with the enemies of Islam in the very last apocalyptic battle takes place to the north of Aleppo. When Muslims who are under the influence of this imagery see the progress of ISIS toward Dabiq, it makes the prophecy seem real and reminds them of their final opportunity for redemption. The leaders of ISIS employ the hadith to create a sense of urgency for sympathetic Muslims to rush to join the movement. There are a number of geopolitical factors that have contributed to the rise of ISIS and made it popular. Yet the symbolism of certain historical events and theological doctrines, which many Sunnis learn in schools or in seminaries, speaks to Sunni religious psychology where it is vulnerable. It is precisely this vulnerability that shapes the worldview of the leaders and members of ISIS, and which the group exploits.

What is the standing of this hadith? Is it regarded as somewhat eccentric or marginal within the tradition? If not, is there a body of such apocalyptic hadiths, and do we know when they date from?

The hadith about Dabiq is cited in a few important collections of hadith, dating back to the ninth century, and is treated as sound and authentic. But for a variety of reasons, we can say with some confidence that it was fabricated. No duel between the Antichrist and Christ exists in the Qur'an—this end-of-time battle is very much a Christian vision, of which Muslims would have first become aware when they broke out of Arabia, and some Christians started to treat their arrival as a prelude to the Antichrist and the Day of Judgment. All of this postdates the time of Muhammad. There is a version of Gog and Magog in the Qur'an (18.94–97), but it derives from earlier Jewish sources. In this hadith, you find the much later idea of an Antichrist—the term in Arabic is *Dajjal*, a literal translation of "Antichrist"—which

Muslims could have no way of understanding until they arrived in regions where this phantasm was already being invoked, but which they then turned around and applied to the Byzantine foe.

Are there other such hadiths?

The books of hadith are classified according to particular topics: so there is one about prayers, there is one about jihad, there is one about the signs of the end of time, in which you invariably find the hadith about Dabiq. But there are plenty of other apocalyptic texts, with different versions of the end-time. Some put a battle between Christ and Antichrist not in Dabiq, but in Jerusalem or Damascus. Others, plainly dating from the Crusades, speak of the Byzantines landing in Acre to attack the Muslims. The Crusaders were not the Byzantines, but if the texts used the Arabic term for them, *faranj*, it would be clear this is an anachronism, since no faranj existed at the time of the Prophet. So instead they substitute the Arabic word for Byzantines (*Rum*), to make it sound as if this was a genuine prophecy from Muhammad. These hadiths were not prized by scholars; they were a kind of curiosity. Sunni scholars were extremely curious, so they read the apocalyptic literature, which was widely known but not highly evaluated in terms of rigorous standards.

So what was its status?

Islam is very much like Judaism: you might believe in the coming of the messiah, but you do not want to deal with it as a reality—you will always push it into the future. You have the same kind of attitude among the Sunnis—no scholar ever sat down and tried to assess these hadiths: there was no urgency to do so. They were just transmitted, and came to form a legitimate body of hadiths within the major compilations.

Do we have any clue as to why Dabiq was selected in the hadith which ISIS invokes?

If we go north of Aleppo, there is a wide plain on which Dabiq—today a hamlet of 3,000 souls—is located, and a little bit beyond it you hit the mountains of southern Anatolia. So geographically, Dabiq lay on the borderline between the Umayyad and Byzantine empires in the seventh and eighth centuries, just where the eschatological imagination would logically place a war at the end of time. Actually, the hadith names two possible sites for this showdown: either Dabiq or Aʿmaq, a valley to the west of Dabiq. But it was Dabiq that stuck. Curiously, ISIS news agency is named Aʿmaq, and its magazine *Dabiq*.

Before ISIS, did anybody make much use of this or other apocalyptic hadiths?

Sure. Throughout the Crusader period, there are scholars who start picking up on apocalyptic hadiths. Ibn ʿAsakir (d. 1174), a Damascene scholar who wrote a massive history of the city in eighty volumes, included a hundred-page biography of Jesus—I have edited this biography—that recounts close to thirty hadiths about the coming back of Jesus. He did not mention the hadith about Dabiq, because he was in Damascus, and the front against the Crusaders lay to the west of where he was. He would have listed Dabiq if they were coming from the north. He listed instead hadiths that locate that battle in Damascus or Jerusalem. Generally, these hadiths become popular in times that give rise to apocalypticism.

Why should Raqqa be a good jumping-off spot for getting to Dabiq? It looks as if it is in the middle of the country.

ISIS is actually after Aleppo. You cannot attack Aleppo unless you have a strong city where you can regroup, and build up your forces, and Raqqa is the only major city to the east of Aleppo. Everywhere else there are small villages that do not provide enough cover from the Syrian army or other forces.

Does ISIS ever attack the Saudis, as al-Qaeda has done?

They have made some attacks in Saudi Arabia, but mostly they were against Shiʿi targets. They have not yet launched a stellar attack within Saudi Arabia. A lot of Saudi money is flowing to ISIS, as well as Saudi recruits and public solidarity. But ISIS is at this point an organization to which every major intelligence service in the region has some connection—definitely the Saudis, and on the other side the Syrian regime and the Iraqi regime. The Turks gave ISIS a lot of facilities, even now that ISIS is blowing up places in Turkey. Many regimes think they can benefit from ISIS, either to fight as their proxy, or, as in the case of Assad, to scare the West and keep his regime afloat.

Would it be correct to think that the novelty—and recruiting attraction—of ISIS as a mutation of contemporary Wahhabi Salafism is its aim to establish a territorial state and proclaim a caliphate? Does not this ambition, in principle at least, set it radically at odds with the kingdom of Sa'ud?

In some sense, yes. ISIS has already broken with a lot of contemporary Salafis on the issue of declaring the caliphate. Some Salafis do not like this, because in their view the time is not ready for the caliphate. There is tremendous division among them on the issue. Even when al-Qaeda was leading the charge of Islamic terrorism, it did not dare to declare a caliphate. The leaders of ISIS realize the religious significance of the move. On the one hand, it reminds the Muslims of the Golden Age of Islam when it conquered and dominated the world and seemed invincible. On the other hand, it accentuates the sense of shame at Muslim disunity and subjugation by Western power, culture, and ideology. Declaring the caliphate is therefore a move that underlines the message that unity is the only way for Muslims to regain their power and pride.

In Sunni religious discourse, the Sunni must obey the caliph. We know from history that this was rarely the case. But in the realm of religious and political theory, most Sunni scholars have argued that Sunnis do not have the right to revolt against their caliph. The most they can do is preach if the caliph does something wrong. Shi'ism also teaches that Shi'is must obey their imams. So when ISIS declares the caliphate and appoints its leader as caliph of Islam, its objective is that Sunnis must hasten to join ISIS. Otherwise they will become lapsed Muslims. It also means that the Sunni Muslims must revolt against their own governments because these regimes are no longer Islamic. Here we see the fatality of the empowerment of Ibn 'Abd-ul-Wahhab and his fanatics by the House of Sa'ud. Wahhabism has reached a stage where it is now undermining the political and religious legitimacy of the Saudi royal family.

Is there a Shi'i equivalent to Salafism?

Hezbollah and the religious ideology of the Iranian regime. The difference is that the message is not broadcast—it is kept within a closed circle. Why are Hezbollah and Iran now involved in Syria? Because of a belief that those who are fighting to topple the Syrian regime will fight them next unless they join forces with Assad. It is the same logic, except here it is pursued by Shiʿis. Hezbollah's grip on the Lebanese Shiʿi community was only cemented when they assassinated a large number of Shiʿi ideological opponents. The Muslim world is now gripped in the utter futility of a murderous conflict between these militant ideologies. It is a tragedy.

If I may add a few personal words, it is difficult to visit Lebanon these days because sectarianism has reached an unprecedented level, much worse than during the civil war of 1975–1991. It is very common to hear members of one sect cursing other sects. I come from a Sunni village in a predominantly Christian area of southern Lebanon, and grew up in a multireligious neighborhood in Beirut. I have very close friends from all sects and am shaped by the rich multicultural aspect of Lebanese society, so much so that I do not see myself confined by any religious affiliation. This is how I was brought up. At no point did my father or mother (who are religious) tell me that I could not befriend a Shiʿi or a Christian.

Lebanese today are forced into their sectarian affiliations. My uncle, a professor of chemistry who lived in a predominantly Shiʿi neighborhood of Beirut and had lots of Shiʿi friends, has now moved to a predominantly Sunni area. My other uncle, who lived in an area that became predominantly Shiʿi, is also now living in a predominantly Sunni area. They moved because they do not feel secure. My closest friend is a Shiʿi who spent all his life in a Sunni area. There, he is a child of the neighborhood—everybody knows him. Now the area has lots of Salafis, it is not safe in the same way for his wife and children, so he had to leave for a part of Beirut where it is a bit more secure. It is an incredibly depressing scene. Yet, obviously, Lebanon is still a little better than the mayhem in Syria, or in Iraq where some lunatic can walk in and blow himself up, irrespective of who is there.

Glossary

Abbasids: a dynasty of caliphs who ruled the Muslim world starting in 750. They traced their genealogy to ʿAbbas, the uncle of Prophet Muhammad. They championed **Sunnism**, and their power dwindled from the tenth century, becoming more symbolic than actual. Their rule ended when the Mongols sacked Baghdad in 1258. Between 1258 and 1517, descendants of the last Abbasid caliph moved to Cairo and became puppet caliphs for the **Mamluk** sultans.

ʿ**Abd-el-Malik:** one of the most important **Umayyad** caliphs. He ruled between 685 and 705, and left a huge religious legacy, including the building of the Dome of the Rock in Jerusalem.

Abu Hanifa (d. 767): see **Hanafis**.

Afghani, Jamal al-Din (d. 1897): Muslim reformer who originally came from Iran, and lived some of his life in France and Egypt. He was a very popular figure among Muslim modernists in the late nineteenth and early twentieth centuries.

Ahmad ibn Hanbal (d. 855): see **Hanbalis**.

Ahmadiyya: a sect that originated in India in the nineteenth century with a **Sunni** scholar named Mirza Ghulam Ahmad (d. 1908), who declared himself a prophet and the Messiah. They were persecuted by other Sunnis, which pushed them to develop as an ecumenical movement with hope to reconcile Sunnism and **Shiʿism**. Today, they exist as an independent sect, and are officially persecuted in Pakistan and other Muslim countries.

ʿAlawis: a Shiʿi sect, also known as Nusayris, that originated from **Twelver Shiʿism** in the ninth century, and only acknowledges the first eleven **imams**. Its theology blends elements from different religions, and holds excessive views of ʿAli as a deity. Today, it has adherents in Syria, Lebanon and Turkey.

Alevis: a **Twelver Shiʿi** ethnic group who live in Turkey today and historically inhabited the region bordering Turkey and Iran. Also known as the Qizilbash or redheaded people (for the red turbans they used to wear), the Alevis were occasionally persecuted by the **Sunni Ottomans** on suspicion of collaboration with the **Shiʿi Safavids** in Iran.

Almohads: a dynasty of militant Berber caliphs in North Africa who toppled the **Almoravids** and took over their empire. Their rule was effectively reduced to Marrakesh and eliminated in 1269. The Almohads were **Sunnis**, following the **Zahiri** school.

Almoravids: a dynasty of militant Berber rulers who rose to power in Morocco in 1062 and controlled western Algeria and parts of Spain until 1147. They were **Sunnis**, following the **Maliki** school.

Ashʿari (d. 936): a **Sunni** theologian whose disciples established a school of theology named after him (Ashʿarism), which is very widespread among Sunnis.

Ayyubids: a dynasty of **Sunni** sultans who ruled Syria, Egypt, western Arabia and parts of south-eastern Turkey and northern Iraq between 1171 and 1250. The dynasty's founder was **Saladin**.

Azhar: a college to teach and train religious scholars and propagandists originally established in Cairo by the **Shiʿi Fatimids**, and converted by **Saladin** in 1171 into a Sunni seminary. It is one of the most prestigious and influential religious seminaries in the Muslim world.

Baath Party: a pan-Arab socialist movement started by Michel Aflaq (an Arab Christian) and others in 1947; it swept to power in Syria in 1963 and in Iraq in 1968.

Bukhari (d. 870): a scholar of **Hadith** who compiled one of the most important hadith collections that **Sunnis** use as foundational resources for Islamic law and religious thought.

Buyids: a dynasty of **Shiʿi** sultans who ruled western Iran and Iraq between 945 and 1048. The **Sunni Abbasids** started their political decline under the Buyids.

Dawud al-Zahiri (d. 884): founder of the **Zahiri** school of **Sunni** law. He flourished in Baghdad, but his school became popular in western North Africa and Muslim Spain.

Druzes: a **Shiʿi** sect that originated from **Ismaʿilism** in the eleventh century. They developed their own syncretistic theology by drawing on Islamic and non-Islamic texts, which are preserved by a group of religious elders who provide religious guidance to the community. In this respect, the Druzes do not adhere any more to the rule of the **imam**. Today, they are dispersed in Lebanon, Syria, Israel, and Jordan.

Fatima: the daughter of Muhammad who was married to ʿAli. She is the mother of **Husayn**, and the **Fatimids** took their name from her.

Fatimids: a dynasty of **Isma'ili** caliphs who ruled Tunis in 909, and occupied most of North Africa and Sicily, then conquered Egypt in 969 and Syria in the years after. They established Cairo and made it their capital. They were eliminated in 1171 by **Saladin**.

Faysal (d. 1933): son of Sharif Husain, the last ruler of Mecca and western Arabia. Faysal was the major figure of the Arab revolt against the **Ottomans** during the First World War, and became king of Iraq (1921–1933) under the British mandate.

Ghaznawids: a dynasty of **Sunni** Turkic warlords who established themselves in Afghanistan, eastern Iran, parts of Central Asia, and what is today Pakistan between 977 and 1186. They were notorious for pillaging Hindu and Buddhist temples—a policy that was extensively pursued under their most notorious ruler Mahmoud of Ghazna (d. 1030)—leaving a horrible legacy in South Asia that still impacts Muslim relations with other Indian religious communities to this very day.

Glubb, J.B. (d. 1986): British general who served in Iraq between 1920 and 1930, and then transferred to Jordan where he became commander of the Bedouin division and in 1939 commander of the Jordanian army (until 1956). Known as Glubb Pasha, he was very influential in Jordanian political and military life.

Hadith: generally, the words attributed to Prophet Muhammad and his companions. They are collected in large volumes (there is no single collection that has them all). Hadith plays a major role in shaping the **Sunna** of Muhammad, and thus Islamic **Shari'a**.

Hamdanids: a dynasty of **Twelver Shi'i** rulers who controlled northern Syria, south-eastern Turkey and parts of north-western Iraq between 890 and 1102 when they were eliminated by the **Isma'ili Fatimids**. Their most important figure was the famous

Sayf al-Dawla (d. 967) whose court featured major philosophers and poets of the time and left a great legacy in Arabic and Islamic culture.

Hanafis: one of the schools of **Sunni** law, named after Abu Hanifa (d. 767), who was chief judge of the city of Kufa (when it was the capital of the **Abbasid** Empire). It is very popular in Turkey, Central Asia, Afghanistan, Pakistan, and India.

Hanbalis: one of the schools of **Sunni** law, named after Ahmad ibn Hanbal (d. 855). It is the only school in Sunnism that has its own theology, and has always been very hardline and militant. The Hanbalis tend to be literalists and emphasize adherence to the dictates of the **Sunna** and the Qur'an, which, in their opinion, was how the noble predecessors (*al-salaf al-salih*) practiced Islam. **Wahhabism** is a branch of the Hanbali school, and most **Salafis** today belong to the Hanbali school or adhere to Hanbali theology.

Hashimis: the dynasty that has ruled modern Jordan since King Abdullah I (d. 1951), who was the son of the last ruler of western Arabia, Sharif Husain. The Hashimis trace their genealogy back to the Prophet Muhammad.

Hijra: the migration of the Prophet Muhammad and his followers from Mecca to Medina in 622. The move to Medina triggered major transformations in the movement that he was forming and reshaped its religious message. Hijra also refers to the Islamic calendar.

Houthis: a powerful **Zaydi** political and religious family in Yemen who, since the 2000s, has been leading a military and political takeover of power in the country.

Husayn (d. 680): son of caliph 'Ali and grandson of Prophet Muhammad. He was killed by an **Umayyad** army in Karbala

(Iraq) in 680. He is the most influential religious figure for **Twelver** and **Isma'ili Shi'is** (in many ways comparable to Jesus).

Ibn Qayyim al-Jawziyya (d. 1350): a very influential medieval **Hanbali** scholar who was the disciple of **Ibn Taymiyya**, and whose works are very popular among **Sunni Salafis**.

Ibn Taymiyya (d. 1328): one of the most notorious militant scholars in Islamic history. He was a **Hanbali**, and lived most of his life in Damascus. He wrote many works that **Sunni Salafis** today, especially jihadists, consider bases for their militancy and violence.

Imam: the title given to **Shi'i** religious leaders who are descendants of the first imam 'Ali, the cousin of Muhammad. As imams, they are granted divine powers to explain Islam to their communities and lead them (which according to the sect, can be either religiously or both religiously and politically). In some Shi'i sects (**Twelvers**), the line of imams ceased in the late ninth century with the disappearance of the twelfth imam. So deputy imams rule on behalf of the absent imam. In other sects (**Zaydis** and **Isma'ilis**), active imams still lead their communities (e.g., the Aga Khan as imam of the Isma'ilis). The word in Arabic and Islamic languages means "leader," and can be used as such by **Sunnis** to indicate a Sunni cleric who has a high religious status but without any theological grounding.

Isma'ilism: the second largest **Shi'i** sect and historically the most significant one. At one point, under the **Fatimids**, they dominated Syria, Egypt, and North Africa, but their power was eliminated by the **Sunni Ayyubids** in the twelfth century. Losing official patronage and facing occasional persecutions, the Isma'ilis were pushed to the peripheries of the Muslim world, especially India where the majority today comes from. Their spiritual leader (**imam**) is called the Aga Khan.

Ja'far al-Sadiq (d. 765): the sixth **Shi'i imam** who was extremely important in the early development of Shi'i religious thought and legal practice. He developed the theology of *taqiyya* (dissimulation) to allow his followers to flourish under the yoke of proto-**Sunni** rule. His disciples collected his legal opinions, which gave rise to the Ja'fari school, the only Shi'i school of law acknowledged by **Sunnism**.

Jizya: the tax that Islamic law imposes on non-Muslims, especially Christians and Jews.

Khomeini (1902–1989): the most important figure of the Iranian Revolution of 1979, which enabled him to play a key role in the religious and political life of Iran and the Middle East, and which extends beyond **Twelver Shi'ism**. He is often called Imam Khomeini, but he is not an imam in the classical Shi'i sense. He is considered by his followers as deputy imam acting on behalf of the absent imam.

Madhhab: a term used to designate each school of law in Islam that defines for its adherents the **Shari'a** of God and the way to follow it.

Malik ibn Anas (d. 795): see **Malikis**.

Malikis: one of the schools of **Sunni** law, named after Malik ibn Anas (d. 795). It is popular in North Africa, and among North African immigrant communities in Europe.

Mamluks (1250–1517): a dynasty of **Sunni** (**Shafi'i**) sultans who ruled the Middle East between 1250 and 1517, when they were eliminated by the **Ottomans**. They were originally recruited as slaves for the army, and some rose in the ranks and were manumitted and became sultans. Except for a few cases, the Mamluks did not adopt hereditary rule. They sponsored a renaissance that left its mark on learning, architecture, culture, religion, and commerce in the Middle East and the Mediterranean world.

Marabouts: the name given to Sufi movements in West Africa. Marabouts blend Islamic and African religious practices and rituals, including music, and their ranks range from wandering mystics to well-established scholars.

Maturidi (d. 944): a **Sunni** theologian whose disciples established a school of theology named after him (Maturidism). It is widespread among Turks and Muslims in Central Asia, and also popular in India and Pakistan.

Mawdudi, Abu al-A'la (1903–1979): a notorious **Sunni** thinker who was born in India and formed the Jama'at-e Islami, and later moved with his followers to Pakistan in 1947. He was a very prolific author and is considered by many as the ideologue of political Islam, and is also an inspirational figure for such militants as **Sayyid Qutb** of Egypt and the Taliban.

Mishna: the teaching of rabbinic Judaism that is considered as the oral Torah and is fundamental for Jewish law. The Mishna was codified as a book in the early third century by Rabbi Yehuda Ha-Nasi, who lived in Roman Palestine.

Mosaddegh, Muhammad (1882–1967): prime minister of Iran between 1951 and 1953. He pursued political, administrative, and economic reforms that led to his removal in a coup orchestrated by Britain and the USA. The downfall of Mosaddegh fueled anti-Western sentiments among Iranian intelligentsia and society at large, and became one of the factors that contributed to the Iranian Revolution in 1979.

Mourides: a religious brotherhood that was established in 1883 in Senegal by the **Marabout** mystic Amadou Bamba (1850–1927).

Keeping a distance from politics, the Mourides have emerged as a major economic power in West Africa.

Mufti: title of a Muslim scholar who issues fatwas or religious edicts. In some Muslim countries, the function is restricted to the highest religious authority who alone has the right to issue fatwas (in countries with a diverse Muslim population such as Lebanon, there is a mufti for each Muslim sect). But since the mufti's authority derives from political power rather than a religious mandate, other scholars issue fatwas as well. In many countries, the mufti holds a governmental post equivalent to a vizier.

Muhammad 'Ali (d. 1849): the powerful ruler of Egypt between 1801 and 1849. He was Albanian by origin, and was dispatched to Egypt by the **Ottomans**, but ruled autonomously and established what became known as the Khedive Dynasty that ruled Egypt and parts of Sudan until 1952, when the last king Faruq was deposed by a palace coup led by Egyptian army officers including Nasser. Muhammad 'Ali was a major force who started the process of modernization in Egypt.

Mutawakkil (r. 847–861): an **Abbasid** caliph whose major accomplishment is the sanctioning of five schools of law as the only legitimate schools in **Sunnism**. This act brought to an end the existence of other schools and closed the door on any possible new ones. It is often misinterpreted as the closure of *ijtihad* in Sunnism.

Mutawakkils: a dynasty of **Zaydi Shi'i imams** who ruled Yemen between 1918 and 1962.

Mu'tazilas: a famous school of rational theology in medieval Islam. It originated in the eighth century as a loose movement but crystallized around a fixed theology in the ninth century. Its members were mostly **Sunnis**, but due to systematic persecution in the eleventh and twelfth centuries, they became outcasts in Sunnism. Their teachings were borrowed by **Twelver** and **Zaydi Shi'is**, and thus constitute the foundation elements for the theological beliefs of these groups.

Nureddin (d. 1171): a **Sunni** sultan who ruled Syria between 1154 and 1171. He started the process of Sunnification of Syria and Egypt, which ultimately led to Sunnis becoming the majority during **Ottoman** times. He was succeeded by his general **Saladin**.

Nusayris: see 'Alawis.

Ottomans: a dynasty of **Sunni (Hanafi)** sultans who ruled an empire that stretched from the Adriatic Sea to Iraq, and from Ukraine to Yemen and Sudan. They originally came from Central Asia, and were among the Turkic tribes that joined the **Seljuk** invasion of the Muslim world. They inhabited Anatolia and emerged in the fourteenth century as a major power, capturing Constantinople in 1453 and occupying Syria and Egypt in 1516 and 1517, after which they claimed the title of caliph. The nineteenth century witnessed major disintegration of the Ottoman Empire, and the First World War reduced it to what is today Turkey. The last Ottoman caliph was eliminated by Ataturk in 1924.

Pan-Islamism: a range of modernist movements that started in the nineteenth century, aiming to create a political and religious unity among all Muslims in order to face the political, economic and cultural hegemony of Europe. Today, many militant jihadists aspire, through militancy, to achieve a form of pan-Islamic unity.

Philby, H. St. John (d. 1960): a powerful British bureaucrat who served in British colonial offices in Iraq, Palestine, and Arabia.

He became a close advisor to King Abd-ul-'Aziz Ibn Saud (r. 1902–1953), and supposedly converted to Islam in 1930. He played an important role in introducing Western oil companies to Saudi Arabia and lobbying on behalf of the Saudis in British colonial circles.

Qasim al-Rassi (d. 860): the most important **Zaydi Shi'i** theologian and jurist who defined the contour of Zaydi theology and jurisprudence. He lived most of his life near Medina, and his grandson Imam Yahya (d. 911) moved to Yemen in 897 and established a Zaydi dynasty (the Rassis), which allowed for a large Zaydi presence that exists there until today.

Qutb, Sayyid (1906–1966): the most inspirational figure for militant **Sunnism** today. His *Milestones* and *Social Justice in Islam* are the two most significant books for modern jihadists and **Salafis** in general. Qutb declared all Muslims to be living in an age of religious ignorance (Jahiliyya), and this led to his execution by the regime of Nasser in 1966.

Safavids: a dynasty of **Twelver Shi'i** shahs who ruled Iran between 1501 and 1736. For a long time they were locked with the **Ottomans** in a battle over Iraq and eastern Anatolia. The Safavids championed and promoted Twelver Shi'ism, a policy that led to Shi'is becoming the overwhelming majority in Iran.

Saladin: the most famous sultan of Islam. He founded the **Ayyubid** dynasty and ruled between 1171 and 1191. He achieved sainthood status after defeating the Crusaders at the Battle of Hattin and liberating Jerusalem in 1187.

Salafism: a designation that refers to several modern **Sunni** movements, ranging from jihadi militants to pacifists, who advocate the need to return to the practices of the *salaf* (predecessors).

According to these groups, the *salaf*—who include the Prophet Muhammad, some of his companions, and a few later scholars —were the perfect Muslims and their Islam was the purest. In recent decades, Salafis are very active in proselytization to fellow Muslims (whom they consider lapsing Muslims) and non-Muslims alike. They also are very vocal and confrontational.

Sanusiyya: a **Sunni** religious reform movement that was established in 1837 in Mecca by an Algerian Sufi called Muhammad al-Sanusi (d. 1859). He relocated to what is today Libya, and through jihad the movement spread to parts of western Sudan and Mali, and was very effective in military resistance to Italian, French, and British colonial ventures in Libya, Egypt, and Saharan Africa. When Libya gained complete independence in 1951, King Idris I, a member of the Sanusi family, was chosen to rule the country; he was later deposed in 1969 by a coup led by Colonel Muammar Gaddafi (d. 2011).

Seljuks: a dynasty of **Sunni** Turkic warlords from Central Asia who invaded the Muslim world starting in the eleventh century, occupied Baghdad in 1055, and put an end to the **Shiʻi Buyid** dynasty. They imposed themselves for close to two centuries as the most feared sultans of Islam, and pursued a policy of Sunnification against mostly Shiʻi groups, especially in Iraq and Iran.

Shafiʻi (d. 820): see **Shafiʻism**.

Shafiʻism: one of the important schools of **Sunni** law, named after Shafiʻi (d. 820). It is mostly present in the Arab Middle East, Yemen, and South Asia.

Shah Waliyullah (d. 1762): a powerful Indian reformer from Delhi, who had a major impact on **Sunni** religious renewal movements in India and South Asia.

Shahada: attestation of faith in Islam. There is a **Sunni** shahada and a **Shiʿi** shahada: *There is no god but God and Muhammad is the messenger of God* (said by Sunnis), and *There is no god but God, Muhammad is the messenger of God, and ʿAli is the friend of God* (said by Shiʿis). It is also uttered at the time of conversion to Islam.

Shariʿa: the body of Islamic law. It is defined differently according to **Sunnis** and **Shiʿis**, and within each of these sects. The Shariʿa is derived from a variety of sources, which, depending on each sect or sub-sect, includes the **Sunna** of Muhammad and his major companions, the words of the **imams** (for Shiʿis), and the Qurʾan.

Shiʿism: the second largest sect of Islam. It is divided into several sub-sects that include **Twelvers, Ismaʿilis, Zaydis, Druzes, ʿAlawis,** and **Alevis.** The Shiʿis emphasize the rule of **imams** who were divinely selected to lead the Muslim community after the death of the Prophet Muhammad. They currently represent around 20 percent of Muslims.

Sira: the genre of Islamic historical literature that focuses on the life of the Prophet Muhammad.

Sunna: the life and acts of the Prophet Muhammad and his companions. It has a tremendous significance as the most important source of **Shariʿa** for **Sunnis,** and is even important for **Shiʿis** as well (Shiʿis have their own version of the Sunna). The corpus of Sunna is scattered in a variety of works, including **hadith** compilations, books of *Sira*, and works of Qurʾanic exegesis.

Sunnism: the largest sect of Islam. It represents around 75 percent of Muslims worldwide and is divided into five sub-sects: **Hanafis, Malikis, Shafiʿis, Hanbalis,** and **Zahiris.** The **Ahmadiyya** Muslims originated from Sunni Islam in north-western India in the nineteenth century, but consider themselves above the sectarian Sunni–Shi'i divide.

Tabari (d. 923): one of the most important Sunni scholars of early Islam. He wrote a very authoritative book of history, widely known as the *History of Tabari*, and also a very authoritative exegesis of the Qur'an, widely known as *Tafsir of Tabari*.

Twelver Shi'ism: the largest sub-sect of **Shi'ism**. Its followers adhere to the teachings of twelve imams, the last of whom disappeared in 874 and is supposed to return before the Day of Judgment. Since then, the community is led by deputy imams who rule on behalf of the last imam. It is predominantly present in Iran, Iraq, Lebanon, north-eastern Saudi Arabia, and Bahrain.

Umayyads: a dynasty of caliphs who ruled the Muslim world from Damascus between 661 and 750. They played a fundamental role in the spread of the Islamic world through conquests (Spain, Central Asia, and what is today Pakistan) and the consolidation of Arabic as the official language and Islam as the official religion of the empire.

Wahhabism: a militant **Hanbali** religious movement formed in Central Arabia by Ibn 'Abd-ul-Wahhab in the eighteenth century. It made a pact with the House of Sa'ud, which is its official sponsor, and is the spearhead of militant Islam today.

Zahiris: one of the schools of law of **Sunnism**. It is named after **Dawud al-Zahiri** (d. 884), and used to be popular in North Africa and Muslim Spain. Its followers today consist of an insignificant number in Morocco and Pakistan.

Zaydis: a sect of **Shi'ism** that was very popular in early Islam, but its numbers dwindled starting in the eleventh century, and its followers survive to this day mostly in Yemen.

Zoroastrianism: one of the world's oldest religions, it is named after Zarathustra who lived approximately 1,500 years before the Common Era. It was the imperial Sassanid religion at the time of the emergence of Islam. It blends elements of dualism and monotheism, and it has been generally treated in Islamic law as a protected religion under the **jizya** system. There has been renewed persecution of Zoroastrians since the Iranian Revolution, and an active community has existed for a long time in western India, where today most of the Zoroastrians are found.

Short Bibliography

Anderson, Perry. *The New Old World*. London: Verso, 2009.

An-Na'im, Abdullahi A. *Toward an Islamic Reformation: Civil Liberties, Human Rights, and International Law*. Syracuse, NY: Syracuse University Press, 1990.

Blankinship, Khalid Y. *The End of the Jihâd State: The Reign of Hishâm ibn 'Abd-el-Malik and the Collapse of the Umayyads*. Albany, NY: SUNY Press, 1994.

Crone, Patricia. "Jihad: Idea and History." *OpenDemocracy* (1 May 2007).

Déroche, François. *Qur'ans of the Umayyads: A First Overview*. Leiden: Brill, 2014.

Donner, Fred M. *Muhammad and the Believers: At the Origins of Islam*. Cambridge, MA: Harvard University Press, 2010.

Eddé, Anne Marie. *Saladin*. Trans. J.M. Todd. Cambridge, MA: Harvard University Press, 2011.

Irwin, Robert. *Dangerous Knowledge: Orientalism and Its Discontents*. Woodstock: Overlook Press, 2006.

Al-Jabri, Mohammad Abed. *The Formation of Arab Reason: Text, Tradition and the Construction of Modernity in the Arab World.* London: I.B. Tauris, 2011.

Kandil, Hazem. *Inside the Brotherhood.* Malden, MA: Polity Press, 2015.

Kennedy, Hugh. *The Prophet and the Age of the Caliphates: The Islamic Near East from the Sixth to the Eleventh Century.* London: Longman, 2014.

Kepel, Gilles. *Jihad: The Trail of Political Islam.* Trans. A.F. Roberts. Cambridge, MA: Harvard University Press, 2002.

Khalidi, Tarif. *Images of Muhammad: Narratives of the Prophet in Islam Across the Centuries.* New York: Doubleday, 2010.

Knight, Michael Muhammad. *The Taqwacores.* Brooklyn, NY: Autonomedia, 2004.

Lauzière, Henri. *The Making of Salafism: Islamic Reform in the Twentieth Century.* New York: Columbia University Press, 2015.

Maalouf, Amin. *In the Name of Identity: Violence and the Need to Belong.* Trans. B. Bray. New York: Arcade, 2012.

Mawdudi, Abu al-A'la. *Jihad in Islam.* Lahore: Islamic Publications, 1976.

Mernissi, Fatima. *Women and Islam: An Historical and Theological Enquiry.* Trans. M.J. Lakeland. Oxford: Basil Blackwell, 1991.

Mourad, Suleiman A. and Lindsay, James E. *The Intensification and Reorientation of Sunni Jihad Ideology in the Crusader Period: Ibn 'Asakir (1105–1176) of Damascus and His Age*; with an edition and translation of Ibn 'Asakir's *The Forty Hadiths for Inciting Jihad.* Leiden: Brill, 2013.

Neuwirth, Angelika. *Scripture, Poetry and the Making of a Community: Reading the Qur'an as a Literary Text.* Oxford:

Oxford University Press, and London: Institute of Ismaili Studies, 2014.

Qutb, Sayyid. *Milestones*. Beirut: Holy Koran Publishing House, 1978.

Roy, Olivier. *Holy Ignorance: When Religion and Culture Part Ways*. New York: Columbia University Press, 2010.

Taha, Mahmud A. *The Second Message of Islam*. Trans. A.A. An-Na'im. Syracuse, NY: Syracuse University Press, 1987.

Tolan, John V. *Saracens: Islam and the Medieval European Imagination*. New York: Columbia University Press, 2002.

Van Ess, Josef. *The Flowering of Muslim Theology*. Trans. J.M. Todd. Cambridge, MA: Harvard University Press, 2005.

Wadud, Amina. *Qur'an and Woman: Reading the Sacred Text from a Woman's Perspective*. New York: Oxford University Press, 1999.

Wansbrough, John. *Quranic Studies: Sources and Methods of Scriptural Interpretation*. Oxford: Oxford University Press, 1977.

Index

Aaron, 19
Abbasids, 31, 39, 44, 45, 46, 47, 49,
    56, 57, 58, 59, 108, 138
'Abd-el-Malik, 21, 22, 44, 138
'Abduh, Muhammad, 69, 70
'Abd-ul-'Aziz Ibn Sa'ud, 72, 73, 75,
    76, 79, 148
'Abdullah Ibn Sa'ud, 75
Abode of Islam (dar al-islam), 44, 51
Abode of Peace, 44
Abode of War (dar al-harb), 44, 51
Abraham, in Qur'an, 18
Abu Bakr, 23, 38–9, 43, 53
Abu Hanifa, 23, 108, 138
adultery, punishment for, 24, 112
Afghani, Jamal al-Din, 69, 70, 138
Ahmad, Mirza Ghulam, 139
Ahmad ibn Hanbal, 69, 108, 138, 142
Ahmadiyya school, 109, 139
'A'isha, 53, 54
'Alawai community (a.k.a. Nusayris),
    60–2, 63, 64, 65, 87, 89, 139
alcohol, use of according to Qur'an,
    25, 34
Aleppo, 47, 48, 59, 60, 65, 111, 128,
    129, 132, 133

Alevis, 51, 61–4, 107, 139
Algeria, 113
'Ali, 22, 33, 52–3, 54, 55, 56, 57, 58,
    61, 94, 96, 102
'Alids, 58
Almohads, 111, 112, 139
Almoravids, 111, 139
alms (zakat), payment of, 26
A'maq (news agency), 132
An-Na'im, Abdullahi, 125, 127, 128
Annunciation of Jesus, 16
anthropomorphism, 110
Antichrist, 128, 130, 131
Apocalypse Tapestry, 8
apocalyptic hadith, 128, 129–31,
    132–3
apocalypticism, 74, 115, 128, 129,
    131, 133
apologetics, 127
apostasy, 43, 73, 92, 93, 118, 127. See
    also takfir (apostasy)
Arab conquests, 21, 37, 38, 39, 40,
    41–2, 43, 44, 50
Arabic language
    addition of vowels and dots to
        alphabet, 10

origins of classical Arabic, 12
origins of modern standard
     Arabic, 12
similar shape of multiple letters in
     alphabet, 9
Arabization, 22
Arab Nationalism, 97
Arabo-Islamic conquests, 38
Arabs, God as coming to, 20
Arab Spring, 89–90, 99
Ash'ari, 110, 139
Ash'aris/Ash'arism, 58, 110
Assad, Hafez, 64, 66, 123, 134
Ataturk, Kemal, 63
attestation of the faith (shahada), 21,
     150
Ayyubids, 48, 105, 140
Azhar, 105, 140

Baath Party, 65, 66, 140
Bahrain, 15, 87, 89, 90, 101
Balkan expeditions, 51
Banna, Hassan, 117–18, 119, 120
Battle of Siffin, 54
belief, 20
Bell, Richard, 7
Berbers, 58, 104, 105, 111, 112, 114
Bin Laden, Osama, 48, 92, 99, 120
brotherhoods, 115. See also Muslim
     Brotherhood
Buddhism, 114
al-Bukhari, Muhammad, 36, 140
burial ritual, 27
Buyids, 58, 59, 94, 140
Byzantine Christianity, 21
Byzantine Empire, 39, 43, 44, 45

caliphate, 54, 55, 103, 104, 116, 134,
     135
caliph(s)
     Abu Bakr, 23, 38–9, 43, 53
     'Ali, 53. See also 'Ali
     defined, 22
     Mu'awiya, 53, 54, 55, 102
     'Umar, 23, 53
     'Uthman, 1, 4, 53, 54

chosen people, 17
Christianity
     development of, 31–2
     traditional Sufism and Shi'ism as
          compared to, 107
     as widespread among Arabs, 15
Christians
     Qur'an's reproach of, 18
     references to in Qur'an, 13, 14
conversions, 21, 38, 41, 42, 45, 87, 92
Covenant/covenant, 18, 19, 20, 43
Crone, Patricia, 38, 39, 42
Crusades, 46–9, 85–6

Dabiq, 128, 129, 130, 131, 132, 133
Dabiq (magazine), 129
Dajjal (Antichrist), 130
Damascus, 40, 41, 48, 55, 61, 65, 69,
     73, 76, 83, 84, 85, 89, 111, 131,
     133
dar al-harb (Abode of War), 44, 51
dar al-islam (Abode of Islam), 44, 51
David, house of, 19
Dawud al-Zahiri, 108, 140, 151
Day of Judgment, 26, 28–9, 61, 128,
     129, 130
Dead Sea Scrolls, 4
Dervish orders, 64
Dhu al-Nurayn (nickname for
     'Uthman), 53
dietary restrictions, 23
divorce, 53, 127
Dome of the Rock, 2, 5, 21, 22
Donner, Fred, 14, 15, 16, 20, 37, 40
dormant embryo, theory of, 112
Druzes, 58, 59, 61, 87, 140

Egypt. See also Mubarak; Sadat
     apocalyptic, messianic, and
          militant movements in, 74
     change in logic of raiding in,
          39–40, 41
     committee in producing Qur'an,
          11, 12
     destruction in, 41
     disappearance of Shi'ism in, 105

Fatimids in, 58–9
as intellectual hub of Arab world, 118
Muslim Brotherhood in, 100, 118, 121, 122, 123
Muslim modernists in, 32
Napoleon in, 75–6
ousting of monarchy in, 91
presence of Christians and Jews in, 42
spread of Wahhabism into, 79
Sufism in, 114
use of radical Sunni groups in, 91
End of Time, 28, 107, 130, 131, 132
Erbakan, Necmettin, 124
Erdoğan, Recep Tayyip, 63, 64, 99, 100, 124
eschatological warning, 28. *See also* Day of Judgment; End of Time
Ezra, 18

fasting, 26, 34, 47, 107
Fatah, 92
Fatima, 53, 55, 57, 94, 140
Fatimids, 58, 59, 103–4, 141
Faysal, 141
free will, 25, 35
Front Islamique du Salut (FIS), 113
Fulani Caliphate of Sokoto, 116
futuh (conquests), 43

Gabriel (angel), 61
ghazi (jihadist), 49–50
Ghaznawids, 46, 141
Glubb, J.B., 79, 141
God
    failure of all movements that argued the word of God trumps everybody else's, 24
    of Qur'an as extremely biblical God, 6
    unity and singularity of as major pillar of Islam, 26
Gog and Magog, 130
Golden Age (of Islam), 69
Gospels, 2, 12, 15, 25, 31

Gospel of John, 17
Gospel of Luke, 19
Gospel of Mark, 31
Gospel of Matthew, 19
Great Mosque (San'a), manuscripts found at, 3–4
Gülen movement, 124
Gulf Cooperation Council, 101

hadiths, 33–6, 81, 128, 129–31, 141
Hafsa, 53
Hagar, 19
Hamas, 92, 124
Hamdanids, 59, 60, 142
Hanafi school/Hanafism, 23, 27, 57, 108, 109, 110, 142
Hanbali school/Hanbalis, 57, 58, 68–9, 83, 108, 109, 110, 142
Hariri, Rafik, 80
Hasan, 55
Hashemite monarchy, 66, 78, 80, 101
Hashimis, 141
Haykal, Muhammad Husayn, 30
Hebrew Bible, 2, 17. *See also* Jewish Bible
hereditary rule, 55
heterodoxy, use of term, 105
Hezbollah, 87, 89, 135, 136
Hijazi (script), 3, 4
hijra (immigration), 71, 119, 142
Hinduism, 114
History of Tabari, 151
House of Sa'ud, 73, 75, 78, 79, 99, 135
Houthi, 'Abd-ul-Malik, 98–9
Houthis, 96, 98, 101, 143
Husain, Sharif, 141
Husayn, 55, 56, 73, 94, 140, 142
Hussein, Saddam, 87, 88

Ibadis/Ibadism, 89, 102, 104
Ibn 'Abd-ul-Wahhab, 71, 72, 74, 75, 77, 78, 82, 83, 84–5, 135
Ibn 'Asakir, 133
Ibn Ishaq, 29
Ibn Anas, Malik, 108, 144

Ibn Qayyim al-Jawziyya, 68, 143
Ibn Sa'ud, 'Abd-ul'Aziz, 72, 73, 75,
    76, 79, 148
Ibn Sa'ud, 'Abdullah, 75
Ibn Sa'ud, Muhammad, 72, 78
Ibn Taymiyya, 48, 68, 69, 83–4, 85–6,
    92, 119, 143
Idrisids, 104
Ikhwan, 123
Imam Hussein, 103
Imami Muslim, 27
imams
    defined, 143
    line of, 56–7
    as untouchable, 25
Immaculate Conception, 16
inheritance, 28, 127
Iran
    Abbasid rule in, 59
    Buyid rule in, 94
    conquering of lands in by
        Muslims, 40
    involvement of in Syria, 135
    Iranian Revolution (1979), 87
    Khawarij in, 102
    Khomeini. See Khomeini
    as majority Shi'i, 60
    Muslim Brotherhood outreach
        to, 122
    outreach of to Shi'i groups across
        Muslim world, 98
    overthrow of Shah in, 91
    perception of American pressure
        on, 89
    rivalry of with Saudi Arabia, 102–3
    Safavid dynasty in, 63
    Sufism in, 114
    Sunni paranoia towards, 100
    Twelver version of Shi'ism in, 62
    Zaydis in, 56–7
    Zoroastrianism in, 42
Iraq
    Abbasid rule in, 59
    Buyid rule in, 59, 94
    change in logic of raiding in,
        39–40

classical Arabic as fabricated in,
    12
conquering of lands in by
    Muslims, 40
Khawarij in, 102
as majority Shi'i, 58, 88
northern part as predominantly
    Sunni, 60
presence of Christians and Jews
    in, 40, 42
ruling by Shi'is in, 64–5, 66
Safavids in, 60
southern part as predominantly
    Shi'i, 60
Sufism in, 114
Zaydis in, 94
Isaac, 15–16, 19, 20
Ishmael, 19, 20
ISIS, 48, 73, 89, 99, 128, 129–30,
    132, 133–4
Islam
    credo of, 21
    disagreement on definition of,
        105–6
    fundamental tenets of, 26
    modernist trends in, 125
    steps taken to make it something
        very distinctive, 21
    as very much like Judaism, 132
Islambouli, Lieutenant, 93
Islamic conquests, 38
Islamic jurisprudence, 22–3
Islamic terrorism, 93, 134. See also
    al-Qaeda; ISIS
Islamism, overthrow of Shah in Iran
    as galvanizing contemporary
    Islamism, 91
Islamization, 22
Isma'ilis/Isma'ilism, 56, 58, 59, 104,
    105, 140, 141, 143–4
Israel, 90–2
Israelites, 17
istislah (public good), 112

Jacob, 20
Ja'far al-Sadiq, 56, 57, 108, 144

Ja'fari school, 57, 108
Jahiliyya, 119–24
Al Jazeera, 100
Jesus
    genealogy of, 19
    as having no father in Qur'an, 16
Jewish Bible, 12, 15. *See also* Hebrew
    Bible
Jews
    Qur'an's reproach of, 18
    references to in Qur'an, 13, 14
jihad
    Balkan expeditions seen as, 51
    as collective duty, 44–5
    during Crusader period, 49
    expansionist vision of, 43
    as individual duty, 45, 47
    as not being waged against fellow
        Muslims, 92, 93
    under Ottoman state, 49–50
    pre-emptive vision of, 44
    use of term, 42–3
jizya (tax), 40, 144
Jordan
    as dependent on Saudi Arabian
        handouts, 80
    as extension of Najd, 76
    Hashemite monarchy in, 101
    Muslim Brotherhood in, 123
    spread of Wahhabism into, 79
Joseph, 16, 19
Judaism
    Islam as very much like, 132
    lineage of, 19
    traditional Sunnism as compared
        to, 107
Judgment Day. *See* Day of Judgment

Kandil, Hazim, 120
Kennedy, Hugh, 14, 15, 37–8
Khawarij (Dissenters), 54, 102, 104
Khedive dynasty, 145
Khomeini, 86, 87, 88, 91, 144
Kitchener, 115
Kufic (script), 3
Kuwait, 101

law of inheritance, 28
Lebanon
    'Alawi in, 61–2
    Druzes in, 62
    emergence of Hezbollah in, 87,
        89
    movement of Shi'i scholars from,
        59
    Muslim Brotherhood in, 123
    sectarian affiliations in, 136
    spread of Wahhabism into, 79
    Sunnis in as under spell of
        Salafism, 80
Life of Muhammad (Haykal), 30

madhhab (the way), 106, 108, 144
Maghreb, 103–5, 108, 111
Mahdi, 115
Mahmoud of Ghazna, 46, 141
Maliki school/Malikis, 57, 101, 108,
    109, 111–12, 144
Mamluks, 48, 49, 59, 60, 63, 85, 105,
    144–5
al-Manar (the Lighthouse), 70
Marabouts, 113–14, 145
marriage
    according to Qur'an, 23
    as matter of personal law, 127
    to sisters, 53
Mary, 16, 19, 31
Maturidis/Maturidism, 58, 110, 145
Mawdudi, Abu al-A'la, 86, 88, 91, 145
Mecca
    message of to Muhammad in, 126
    pilgrimage to, as pillar of Islam, 26
    very few original inhabitants as
        staying in, 41
Meccan verses, 5, 7, 13
medieval texts, as full of
    contradictions, 25
Medina
    meaning of jihad in, 43
    message of to Muhammad in, 126
    very few original inhabitants as
        staying in, 41
Medinan verses, 5, 6–7, 13–14

messiah/messianism, 19, 116, 132, 139
Milestones (Qutb), 120
militant Islam, 93, 100, 151. *See also* Salafism; Wahhabism
Mishna, 13, 145
Mongols, 48–9, 86, 92
monotheism, 6, 13, 14, 18, 40, 152
Morsi, Muhammad, 122
Mosaddegh, Muhammad, 87, 145–6
Moses, in Qur'an, 18
Mourides, 114, 115–16, 146
Mu'awiya, 53, 54, 55, 102
Mubarak, Hosni, 93, 120, 121, 122
Mufti, 69, 96, 146
Muhammad, Prophet
    biographical evidence about life of, 29–32
    death of, 1
    disputes about life of, 32–3
    expulsion of from Mecca, 13
    genealogy of, 19–20
    issue of succession after death of, 52–5
    as not literate, 1
    as reflecting tensions of society where religion is felt to have been corrupted, 13
    as unifying Arabia, 38
Muhammad 'Ali, 75, 76, 77, 145
Mukhtar, 'Umar, 112
mullahs, 91, 103
Muslim Brotherhood, 100, 117–20
Muslim reform movements, 117, 125–7
Muslims
    contemporary Muslims as not understanding Islam correctly, 11
    early Muslims as already part of community of believers, not bearers of something very new, 21
    in Medina, 6
    use of term, 20
    variations of, 27

Mutawakkil, 57, 108, 146
Mutawakkils, 96, 97, 146
Mu'tazilas/Mu'tazilism, 95, 146–7
Mu'tazilis/Mu'tazilism, 58, 110
mysticism/mystics, 30, 62, 64, 82, 107, 116

Nag Hamadeh, 4
Najd, 72, 73, 76, 78, 84, 85
Naqshbandi, 116
Nasser, Jamal 'Abd-ul, 97, 119
Nawawi, 81–2
Nimeiry, 127
Nöldeke, Theodor, 7
nomadic conquests, 39
Nour Party, 122
Nureddin of Aleppo, 47–8, 60, 147
Nusayris, 58, 61, 62. *See also* 'Alawai community (a.k.a. Nusayris)

Omani Sultanate, 102
orthopraxy, 27, 107, 108
Ottomans, 49–50, 60, 110, 147

Palestine
    change in logic of raiding in, 39–40
    destruction in, 41
    Muslim Brotherhood in, 124
Palestinians, 91
pan-Arabism, 70
pan-Islamism, 70, 86, 87, 88, 90, 91, 147
pan-Shi'ism, 87, 88, 89
pan-Sunnism, 88–9
papyri, 3
parchment, 3
Paul, theology of, 18, 19
Pentateuch, 25
Persian conquest of 614, 41
Persian Empire, 21, 39, 40
Philby, H. St. John, 79, 147–8
physical anthropomorphism, 110
polytheism, 6, 7, 13
prayer, 26, 44, 107, 118, 131
predestination, 25, 35

Prophets (Hebrew Bible), 17
Protestant Reformation, 125
Protestant trap, 125
Protevangelium of James, 31
proto-Shi'ism, 52, 55, 58, 59
proto-Sunnism, 52, 55, 57, 58, 59

Qadi 'Iyad, 30–1
al-Qaeda, 89, 99, 120, 133, 134
qala (he said), 4
Qasim al-Rassi, 95, 148
Qataris, 100
Qizilbash (redheads), 51
qul (say), 4
Qur'an
    as able to be treated quite flexibly,
        25
    ceremonial role of, 125
    construction of Jesus's ministry as
        depicted in, 16
    contradictions in, 25–6
    date of official canonical text, 7
    as difficult text, 2
    as having grammatical mistakes, 7
    as having several canonically
        sanctioned ways of reading
        of, 10
    language of, 11
    as legitimizing things modern
        Muslims consider
        embarrassing, 125
    limitation of, 126
    mass production and wide
        distribution of, 11
    as not understandable without the
        Sira, 32
    as obsessed with polytheism, 13
    oral traditions behind, 7, 10, 29,
        33
    origins of, 1–3
    parallels to Rabbinical Judaism
        in, 15
    today's version same as one
        produced in 650, 8
    uncompromising stance of against
        all transgressors, 17
    as viewed as miraculous, 7
    Yemeni manuscript of, 4
Quraysh tribe, 6
Qutb, Sayyid, 86, 88, 91, 119, 120,
    148

Rabbinical lore/tradition, 12, 15, 20
rafida (rejectionists), 82
Raqqa, 129, 133
Rida, Rashid, 69–70, 77
ridda (war against apostasy), 43

Saad, 80
Al Sabah dynasty, 101
Sadat, 91–2, 93
Safavids, 51, 60, 63, 107, 148
sahih (sound), 36
Saladin, 48, 60, 104, 105, 140, 141,
    148
Salafi (attachment to predecessors),
    67–8
Salafism, 68–71, 73, 77, 80, 91, 92,
    93, 98, 99, 101, 108, 109, 113,
    117, 118, 120, 121, 122, 134, 135,
    136, 142, 148–9
Saleh, 'Ali, 98
Sanusiyya, 115, 116, 149
Sassanian Empire, 39, 40, 43
Saudi Arabia
    Britain as helping kingdom of into
        being, 79
    campaign of against Yemen, 96
    as champion of pan-Sunnism
        against Iran, 89
    handouts of to Jordan, 80
    lack of stability in, 90
    as reference point for Sunnis, 99,
        100
    rivalry of with Iran, 102–3
    ruling family as apostates, 92–3
    support of to groups such as ISIS,
        99, 134
    view of Muslim Brotherhood,
        122
    Wahhabi movement in, 77
schools. *See also* Ahmadiyya school;

Hanafi school/Hanafism; Hanbali
school/Hanbalis; Ja'fari school;
Maliki school/Malikis; Shafi'i
school/Shafi'is; Zahiri school/
Zahiris
of law (in Islam), 26, 27
many Muslims having no idea
what school of law they
belong, 111
Shi'i school, 57
Sunni schools, 57, 58, 109–10
Seljuks, 94, 95, 110, 147, 149
Seveners (Isma'ili sect), 56
Shafi'i school/Shafi'is, 27, 34, 35, 57,
96, 108, 109, 110, 149
shahada (attestation of the faith), 21,
150
Shah Wali Allah, 74
Shah Waliyullah, 149
Shari'a
alcohol as banned in, 25
application of to matters of
personal law, 127
defined, 150
as defined differently according to
each school of law, 26
each of Sunni divisions as having
its own, 106
flexibility of, 126, 127
Hadith as needed to specify, 34
as Islamic jurisprudence, 22–3
lack of understanding about, 27
as laws, rituals, and practices, 110
as not defined in Qur'an, 27
principles of 'urf and istislah in,
112
punishment for adultery in, 24
on use of alcohol, 25
variations within, 27
Shi'is/Shi'ism
account of villainy of Mu'awiya
and Yazid as part of, 55
on caliphate, 135
considered by Sunnis as rafida, 82
contemporary dynamic of with
Sunnis, 86–8

defined, 150
as developing own shahada,
21–2
differences between Shi'is and
Sunnis, 9
disappearance of in North Africa
after Fatimids, 104–5
as following teachings of imams,
24
as having own versions of the
Sira, 33
original nature of split with
Sunnis, 52–5
origins of, 56, 57, 58–60
Safavids as, 51
schools, 26, 57
sira, 150
Sira (Ibn Ishaq), 29, 31
el-Sisi, General Abdel Fattah, 100,
122
sola scriptura, 32
spiritualism, 107
submission, 20
Sufis/Sufism, 58, 105–8, 110, 111,
113–15
Sunna, 24, 25, 34, 150
Sunnis/Sunnism
on caliphate, 135
contemporary dynamic of with
Shi'is, 86–8
as creation of class of urban elites,
114
defined, 150–1
differences between Sunnis and
Shi'is, 9
Hadith for, 34
idea of compromise at heart of,
81–2
as not practicing carnal unions,
23
original nature of split with Shi'is,
52–5
origins of, 57–8
Ottomans as champions of, 50
as rejecting Shi'is versions of the
Sira, 33

schools, 26, 57, 58, 109–10
Sunna as number-one source of
    guidance for conduct, 24
Syria
    change in logic of raiding in,
        39–40
    involvement of Iran in, 135
    Isma'ili Shi'ism in, 104
    Muslim Brotherhood in, 123–4
    presence of Christians and Jews
        in, 42
    ruling by 'Alawi in, 61, 64–6, 89
    Shi'is in, 59
    spread of Wahhabism into, 79
    Sufism in, 114
Syriac Christianity, 12

Tabari, 69, 151
Tafsir al-Manar, 70
Tafsir of Tabari, 151
Taha, Mahmoud, 125, 126–7, 128
takfir (apostasy), 92, 93, 118, 119
Talha, 54
taqiyya (lying low; dissimulation),
    94, 144
tariqa (the way), 115
Temple of Solomon, 22
Al Thani dynasty, 100
theology of Paul, 18, 19
Trinity, Qur'an as attacking idea of,
    16, 18
Turkey. *See also* Erdoğan
    'Alawi/Alevis in, 61–2
    as first and foremost a country for
        Turks, 64
    Gülen movement in, 124
    Hanafis in, 109, 110
    as opposed to Iran, 64
    spread of Wahhabism into, 79
    Sunnis in, 60

Twelver Shi'is, 58, 59, 62, 87, 94,
    139, 142, 143, 151

UAE, 89, 101, 123
'Ubbad al-Rahman (Worshipers of
    the Merciful), 123
'Umar, 23
Umayyads, 10, 39, 43, 44, 55, 151
umma (Muslim community), 52
unitarian, as describing Meccan parts
    of Qur'an, 5–6
'urf (local customs), 112
Usman dan Fodio, 116
'Uthman, 1, 4, 53, 54
Uzayr, 18

Wahhabism, 69, 70, 71, 73, 74, 75,
    76, 77, 78, 79, 80, 81, 82, 89, 92,
    98, 99, 100, 101, 103, 109, 117,
    120, 134, 135, 142, 151
Wansbrough, John, 3

Yahya, 95
Yazid, 54
Yemen
    Qur'an manuscript from, 4
    Shafi'i school in, 109
    Shi'i–Sunni clash at heart of
        current Saudi campaign in, 96
    Wahhabis in, 99
    Zaydis in, 56–7, 89, 94–6, 98

Zahiri school/Zahiris, 57, 108, 109,
    111, 151
Zarathustra, 152
Zawahiri, Ayman, 120
Zaydis, 56–7, 58, 59, 87, 89, 94–7, 98,
    99, 104, 143, 151
Zoroastrianism, 21, 40, 42, 151–2
Zubayr, 54